MW00962614

Tulane University

New Orleans, Louisiana

Written by Kate Dearing
Edited by Tim Williams

Additional contributions by Omid Gohari,
Christina Koshzow, Chris Mason, Joey Rahimi,
Jon Skindzier, Luke Skurman, Tim Williams, Sylvette Sein

ISBN # 1-59658-135-2
ISSN # 1552-0838

Special thanks to: Babs Carryer, Andy Hannah, Launch-Cyte, Tim O'Brien, Bob Sehlinger, Thomas Emerson, Andrew Skurman, Barbara Skurman, Bert Mann, Dave Lehman,Daniel Fayock, Chris Babyak,The Donald H. Jones Center for Entrepreneurship, Terry Slease, Jerry McGinnis, Bill Ecenberger, Idie McGinty, Kyle Russell, Jacque Zaremba, Larry Winderbaum, Paul Kelly, Roland Allen, Jon Reider, Team Evankovich, Julie Fenstermaker, Lauren Varacalli, Abu Noaman, Jason Putorti, Mark Exler, Daniel Steinmeyer, Jared Cohon, Gabriela Oates, Tri Ad Litho, David Koegler and Glen Meakam.

Bounce Back Team: Sunny Hale, Jeff Garcia

College Prowler™
5001 Baum Blvd.
Suite 456
Pittsburgh, PA 15213

Phone: (412) 697-1390, 1(800) 290-2682
Fax: (412) 697-1396, 1(800) 772-4972
E-mail: info@collegeprowler.com
Website: www.collegeprowler.com

Welcome to College Prowler™

During the writing of College Prowler's guidebooks, we felt it was critical that the information within was unbiased, and that the guides were unaffiliated with any college or university. We think it's important that our readers get honest information and a realistic impression of the student opinions on any campus—that's why if any aspect of a particular school is terrible, we (unlike a campus brochure) intend to publish that fact. While we do keep an eye out for the occasional extremist—the cheerleader or the cynic—we take pride in letting the students tell it like it is. We strive to create a book that's as representative as possible of each particular campus. Our books cover both the good and the bad, and whether the survey responses point to recurring trends or a variation in opinion, these sentiments are directly and proportionally expressed through our guides.

College Prowler guidebooks are in the hands of students throughout the entire process of their creation. Because you can't make student-written guides without the students, we have students at each campus who help write, randomly survey their peers, edit, layout, and perform accuracy checks on every book that we publish. From the very beginning, student writers gather the most up-to-date stats, facts, and inside information on their colleges. They fill each section with student quotes and summarize the findings in editorial reviews. In addition, each school receives a collection of letter grades (A through F) that reflect student opinion and help to represent contentment, prominence, or satisfaction for each of our 20 specific categories. Just as in grade school, the higher the mark the more content, more prominent, or more satisfied the students are with the particular category.

Once a book is written, additional students serve as editors and check for accuracy even more extensively. Our bounce-back team—a group of randomly selected students who have no involvement with the project—are asked to read over the material in order to help ensure that the book accurately expresses every aspect of the university and its students. This same process is applied to the 200-plus schools College Prowler currently covers. Each book is the result of endless student contributions, hundreds of pages of research and writing, and countless hours of hard work. All of this has led to the creation of a student information network that stretches across the nation to every school that we cover. It's no easy accomplishment, but it's the reason that our guides are such a great resource.

When reading our books and looking at our grades, keep in mind that every college is different and that the students who make up each school are not uniform—as a result, it is important to assess schools on a case-by-case basis. Because it's impossible to summarize an entire school with a single number or description, each book provides a dialogue, not a decision, that's made up of 20 different topics and hundreds of student quotes. In the end, we hope that this guide will serve as a valuable tool in your college selection process. Enjoy!

OMID GOHARI ○ CHRISTINA KOSHZOW ○ CHRIS MASON ○ JOEY RAHIMI ○ LUKE SKURMAN ○
Founders of College Prowler™

Table of Contents

By the Numbers............................ **1**

Academics **4**

Local Atmosphere **10**

Safety and Security................... **17**

Computers................................. **22**

Facilities..................................... **27**

Campus Dining.......................... **32**

Off-Campus Dining **37**

Campus Housing **45**

Off-Campus Housing............... **53**

Diversity..................................... **57**

Guys and Girls **62**

Athletics..................................... **68**

Nightlife..................................... **75**

Greek Life **83**

Drug Scene................................. **87**

Campus Strictness **90**

Parking.. **93**

Transportation **97**

Weather....................................**103**

Report Card Summary **107**

Overall Experience **108**

The Inside Scoop....................**111**

Finding a Job or Internship **115**

Alumni Information.................**117**

Student Organizations...........**120**

The Best & Worst....................**126**

Visiting Campus......................**128**

Words to Know........................**132**

Introduction from the Author

Congratulations. If you are reading this book, you are considered (or you consider yourself) to be one of the most intelligent people who are applying to colleges today. With its last freshman class holding an average SAT score in the 1300s and an international reputation as one of the best schools in the nation, Tulane University is a school with a very intelligent student body, and a tough school to get into. If you are reading this book and you don't consider yourself the shiniest crayon in the box, you must be part of a very wealthy family. The total amount for a year's worth of tuition and fees costs more than what some Americans make in an entire year. Tulane campus is littered with Louis Vuitton handbags and designer shoes. A popular Tulane motto that is said among students is "You're either a smart kid here on scholarship or you're rich kid looking for the ultimate party school."

For those of you who don't know, Tulane is located in New Orleans – home of the world famous Mardi Gras celebration, Bourbon Street, countless bars, and a vibrant social scene. With that in mind, if you have any objections to drinking and partying, it's best not to look into Tulane. New Orleans has a very laid-back feel, much different than most big cities in the States. The way I like to put it is that it's like living in France: the drinking age is 18 (if you can get into a club, you can get a drink), and some locals speak French as their first language.

Tulane is considered to be the "Harvard of the South," and is the best college education that Louisiana can offer. It's located about 20 minutes from the French Quarter and downtown. New Orleans is full of art, music, museums, amazing food, and a culture that is unique to the area. The combination of academic knowledge, culture and entertainment is incredible. You're guaranteed to get a great education while having an awesome time living here.

Unlike most college decision books, this is written by me – a Tulane freshman who knows what you are going through and what you are looking for in a college. I've been through orientation and two semesters here. This guide will give you what real students think about the real Tulane. So forget all the rankings and numbers, this is what you really need to know while you decide if you will be a Tulanian forever, or not even consider applying. Good luck with your decision, and happy reading.

Kate Dearing, Author
Newcomb College

By the Numbers

General Information

Tulane University
6823 St. Charles Avenue
New Orleans, LA 70118

Control:
Private

Academic Calendar:
Semester

Religious Affiliation:
None

Founded:
1834

Website:
www2.tulane.edu

Main Phone:
(504) 865-5000

Admissions Phone:
800-873-9283

Student Body

Full-Time Undergraduates:
5,989

Part time Undergraduates:
1,873

Full-Time Male Undergraduates:
3,723

Full-Time Female Undergraduates:
4,139

Female:Male Ratio
52.6%:47.4%

Admissions

Overall Acceptance Rate:
55%

Total Applicants:
14,107

Total Acceptances:
7,801

Freshman Enrollment:
1,684

Yield (% of admitted students who actually enroll):
21.5%

Early Decision Available?
Yes

Early Action Available?
Yes

Early Decision Deadline:
November 1

Early Decision Notification:
December 15

Regular Decision Deadline:
January 1

Regular Decision Notification:
April 1

Must Reply-By Date:
May 1

Applicants Placed on Waiting List:
715

Applicants Accepted From Waiting List:
478

Students Enrolled From Waiting List:
6

Transfer Applications Received:
470

Transfer Students Accepted:
357

Transfer Students Enrolled:
145

Transfer Acceptance Rate:
75.9%

Common Application Accepted?
Yes

Supplemental Forms?
Yes

Admissions Phone:
(800)-873-9283

Admissions Email:
undergrad.admissions@tulane.edu

Admissions Website:
http://tulane.edu/admission.cfm

SAT I or ACT Required?
Either

**SAT I Range
(25th – 75th Percentile):**
1240 – 1420

**SAT I Verbal Range
(25th – 75th Percentile):**
610 – 730

**SAT I Math Range
(25th – 75th Percentile):**
630 – 690

Top 10% of High School Class:
65%

Application Fee:
$55

Financial Information

Full-Time Tuition:
$31,210 per year.

Room and Board:
$7,925

Books and Supplies for class:
$800 per year

Average Need-Based Financial Aid Package:
$25,837
(including loans, work-study, grants, and other sources)

Students Who Applied for Aid:
53%

Students Who Received Aid:
42%

Financial Aid Forms Deadline:
February 1

Financial Aid Phone:
504-865-5723 or (800) 335-3210

Financial Aid E-mail:
finaid@tulane.edu

Financial Aid Website:
http://www.tulane.edu/~finaid/

Academics

The Lowdown On...
Academics

Degrees Awarded:

Associate

Bachelor

Master

Doctorate

Most Popular Areas of Study:

21% business, management, marketing, and related support services, 17% social sciences, 9% engineering, 8% psychology, 7% biological and biomedical sciences

Undergraduate Schools:

Newcomb College

A.B. Freemen School of Business

School of Architecture

School of Engineering

School of Social Work

University College

Men's A&S School

Fulltime Faculty:

747

→

Faculty with Terminal Degree: 98%	**4 Year Graudation Rate:** 62%
Student-to-Faculty Ratio: 9:1	**5 Year Graudation Rate:** 72%
Average Course Load: 13.6	**6Year Graudation Rate:** 74%

Special Degree Options

BSE/MSE 5-Year Degree in Engineering

The BSE/MSE 5-Year Degree in Engineering program is run by the engineering department and the honors program; it results in a B.S. in Engineering or Computer Science and a M.S. in the same field after five years.

Engineering-Master of Business Administration

This is a program to earn a B.S. in Engineering and an MBA after five years.

Bachelor of Science/Arts and Masters Degree in Public Health (BS/MSPH).

This is a program to earn dual degrees in the field of environmental health. During the third year, students enrolled in this program begin to take graduate level courses in the Environmental Health Sciences Department downtown at the SPHTM.

Tulane offers many 4+1 Programs, such as:

The 4+ 1 Neuroscience Program: This M.S. program in Neuroscience provides students with one additional year of graduate level training, beyond the baccalaureate degree.

AP Test Score Requirements

Possible credit for scores of 4 or 5

IB Test Score Requirements
Possible credit for scores of 5 and greater

Academic Clubs
American Institute of Architecture Students

American Marketing Association

American Society of Civil Engineers

Association of Pre-Dental Students

Biomedical Engineering Society, Philosophy Club, Pre-Law Society

Pre-Medical Society

Society of Women Engineers

Spanish and Portuguese Student Association

Tulane University Neuroscience Association (TUNA)

Tulane-Newcomb Art Student Association, Women in Science

Undergraduate Student Government (USG)

Did You Know?

In 1886, Josephine Louise Newcomb founded Newcomb College, the first degree-granting women's college in the nation, to be established as a coordinate division of a university.

There were over 18,000 applications sent in for Tulane's class of 2008!

Best Places to Study
Howard-Tilton Library; the PJ's patio on Willow St.; outside on a sunny day on one of the many quads

Students Speak Out On...
Academics

> "It's evident that most of my teachers have a lot of experience working outside of Tulane in their respected fields. Their international, "real world" examples make the classes interesting."

Q "**When it comes to teachers, it's very hit or miss.** The ones that are good are amazing, and the ones that suck really suck."

Q "The teachers are generally very good. **I have particularly enjoyed my international relations class.**"

Q "**Teachers are not what I expected from such a prestigious school.** Some are downright awful and shouldn't be teachers. Few are enthusiastic. Classes are good because they are so small."

Q "The classes that are taken by choice I usually end up enjoying, but **the ones that I take due to a requirement I don't enjoy as much because they don't spark my interest.** The teachers are pretty decent for the most part."

Q "**The teachers are well read and intelligent**... most of the time."

Q "Take this piece of advice: **research your classes and your teachers before you commit to a schedule.** There's usually more than one section of a class for each course, and different teachers will be better than others. Talk to upperclassmen and find out who they liked and didn't like before you get into a class. If you start to get the feeling that you don't like a teacher, drop the class and take it with someone else or do it another semester. Oh, yeah... and be careful with math courses. It's the worst department at Tulane."

Q "Most of the teachers are good, and I find the classes interesting. However, **there are certain genetics teachers who are evil.**"

Q "I have now attended classes at three universities, and **the Tulane professors have the highest probability of knowing what they are talking about.**"

Q "Many are graduate students or foreign; **on occasion class sparks a little interest.**"

Q "They seem brilliant, but **a lot are 'absent minded professors.'**"

The College Prowler Take On...
Academics

As with any school, you're going to hate some professors and love others. Some of Tulane's faculty members are very influential, both in the academic world and in their particular fields. The accessibility of these professors, however, often depends on class size. At Tulane, you'll find a mixture of small-group classes and huge lectures. The core classes required for most majors and many of the science requirements (chemistry, for example) have classes upwards of 150 students. If you take a foreign language or a class in the 300 or 400 level, however, the class will not exceed 25 students in order to allow for more teacher-student interaction. Many professors of smaller classes let class run outside in one of the many quads on a pretty day.

Contacting professors is usually very easy at Tulane. They are very accessible through the Blackboard (internet) system, email, or office hours. Most are very helpful and friendly when you have a problem or a question with the material. Because of the prestigious name, they do not let just anyone teach at Tulane. Most professors are very intelligent and knowledgeable about their subject. The main problem that many students express is a feeling that faculty don't understand the best way to teach their material, and that this makes classes harder than they have to be. Getting in touch with your professors and TAs is, by far, the best way to overcome such problems.

B

The College Prowler™ Grade on
Academics: B

A high Academics grade generally indicates that Professors are knowledgeable, accessible, and genuinely interested in their students' welfare. Other determining factors include class size, how well professors communicate, and whether or not classes are engaging.

Local Atmosphere

The Lowdown On...
Local Atmosphere

Region:
South

City, State:
New Orleans, LA

Setting:
Urban

Distance from Baton Rouge (LSU):
1.5 hours

Points of Interest:
Bourbon Street
Magazine Street
D-day Museum

Closest Shopping Malls:
Shops at Canal Place
333 Canal St
New Orleans, LA 70130

Riverwalk
1 Poydras St
New Orleans, LA 70130

→

Clearview Mall
4436 Veterans Memorial Blvd
Metairie, LA 70006

Closest
Movie Theatres:
Prytania Theatre
5339 Prytania Street,
New Orleans, LA 70115
(504)891-2787

**Landmark Canal Place
Cinema**
333 Canal Street
New Orleans, LA 70130
(504) 581-5400

AMC Palace 12- Clearview
4486 Veterans Memorial Blvd.
Metairie, LA 70006
(504) 734-2020

**Entergy IMAX at the
Aquarium of the Americas**
1 Canal Street
New Orleans, LA 70130
(800) 774-7394

Major Sports Teams:
Zephyrs (Minor League
Baseball)
Voodoo (Arena Football)
Hornets (Basketball)

City Websites
www.neworleansonline.com
www.nola.com
www.neworleans.com

Did You Know?

5 Fun Facts about Tulane:

- More than 500,000 king cakes are sold each year in New Orleans between January 6 and Fat Tuesday, and another 50,000 are shipped out-of-state via overnight courier.

- An economic study released by the University of New Orleans estimates that Mardi Gras generates more than $840 million annually.

- New Orleans the only U.S. city where French was the predominant language for more than one century.

- New Orleans is often called the "Crescent City" because it was founded on the bend of the Mississippi River. This unusual shape causes locals and visitors to become confused occasionally, as there is no traditional "north, south, east, or west" mode of getting around.

- Many of the tens of thousands of live oak trees that line the streets and boulevards date back to before the Civil War. They have survived hurricanes, droughts, pests, and fires.

Famous People from New Orleans:

Louis Armstrong

Truman Capote

Kordell Stewart

Lillian Hellman

Local Slang

"The Big Easy" – the official nickname for New Orleans, after a contest many years ago.

Carnival – the party season before Mardi Gras; starts on January 6 (the Twelfth Night)

Creole – descendents of French, Spanish, and Caribbean slaves and natives; also come to mean any person whose ancestry derives from the mixed nationalities in the Caribbean.

Doubloons – aluminum coins stamped with the parade krewe's insignia and theme

Fixin' to – means "about to" in local dialect

Lagniappe – something extra that you didn't pay for

Laissez le Bon temp rouler – "let the good times roll"

Students Speak Out On...
Local Atmosphere

"The best way to describe New Orleans is as a developing country. The richest people live 2 blocks from the poorest. There are multiple universities in the area; however, they don't compare to Tulane. Stay away from Audubon Park at night, and make sure to visit the D-Day museum."

Q "I love the atmosphere! It's **warm, friendly, and fun** – you can't get any better than that!"

Q "The atmosphere is **awesome.** I would say that New Orleans is the perfect college town. There's always something going on, things to do, and places to see."

Q "There are **tons of cultural places to visit** and even more fun things to do. There are other universities and a city that draws people that are laidback and looking for a good time."

Q "New Orleans is extremely **laidback and can be a little crazy,** but you can take in as much of the craziness as you want. There are other universities present, but Tulane is the biggest and Tulane students are the ones you usually meet."

Q "There are **a lot of fun and interesting things to do** and see. I love the French Quarter, Audubon Zoo, and the aquarium. The restaurants are amazing."

Q "It's a **top tourist town.** I would stay away from Harrah's Casino – casinos are too expensive for students."

Q "Loyola is right next door, but **Tulane rarely gets involved with other schools.** It's kind of like the snooty university of the South."

Q "The atmosphere in New Orleans is **laid back.** Loyola is right next door. Stay away from the 'hood, and make sure to visit the park (Audubon) and the zoo."

Q "The atmosphere in this town is one which **seems to pressure citizens into extreme drinking habits.** There are other universities present, like Loyola. Stuff to stay away from: being by yourself at night. Stuff to visit: the cemeteries, Magazine Street."

Q "If you feel that **drinking isn't the best social activity**, for the love of God don't make the same mistake that I did. Don't come here!"

The College Prowler Take On...
Local Atmosphere

At any given time, there are people come from all over the country on holiday in New Orleans. There are very few cities in the States that can match New Orleans' abundant culture, quaint architecture, amazing food, and party scene. Whether or not you plan to attend Tulane, it's a great city to visit.

If you like animals, you should check out the Audubon Zoo or the Aquarium. If you're into history, then visit the D-Day museum. Art and music are in abundance here, with cinemas, museums, and theaters all over the place. In terms of sports, New Orleans has football, baseball, and basketball teams to root for. For a more artsy feel, there are plenty of quiet Jazz Cafes and small bookstores all over the city. Local and famous bands come through to perform throughout the year – many musicians and artists make their home in the streets of New Orleans.

If you have a hobby or interest of any kind, you'll find it in this city. There's always something to do or see, be it Voodoo Fest and partying on Frenchman over Halloween, Jazz Fest that's held at the end of the Spring semester, or the world famous Mardi Gras celebration and the month of parades, balls, and parties that it brings to the city; there is always something to look forward to. No matter where you're from, by the end of your first year at Tulane you'll agree that New Orleans is one of the liveliest cities in the world.

The College Prowler™ Grade on

Local Atmosphere: B+

A high Local Atmosphere grade indicates that the area surrounding campus is safe and scenic. Other factors include nearby attractions, proximity to other schools, and the town's attitude toward students

Safety & Security

The Lowdown On...
Safety & Security

of Tulane University Police:
76

of Emergency Phones:
33

Tulane Police Phone:
(504) 865-5200

Safety Services:
24-hour Exterior Door-Locking System

Blue Light Phones

Desk Assistants

Entrance Into Buildings Is By Key or Card

Personal Escort Service

Health Services:
Emergency Contraception

Laboratory For Lab Work/Tests

Nurse Triage Express

Nutrition Services

Pharmacy

Health Center Office Hours

Monday-Friday: 8:30 am-4:30pm

Tuesdays (school year only): 8:30am-6pm

Saturday: 9 am- noon

Sunday: Closed

Summer Hours: 9 am-3 pm

Did You Know?

Tulane Emergency Medical Service (Tulane EMS) is an ambulance service run by students who are basic and intermediate level Emergency Medical Technicians.

Students Speak Out On...
Safety & Security

"Security is excellent on campus, but non-existent off campus. Even just a few blocks off-campus there have been several muggings and sexual assaults this year – almost all were young women walking alone at night."

Q "I always feel safe on campus. It is when I'm off-campus late at night that I feel threatened."

Q "I've heard of bad things happening to other people, but nothing has ever happened to me."

Q "In my experience security has been fine and adequate."

Q "The TUPD isn't the sharpest force, but they do their job well. I don't feel unsafe on campus at all."

Q "I feel safe on campus, and when I'm off campus I don't feel safe if I'm alone."

Q "If you are ever in River Ridge/old Metairie, watch your back. I cannot tell you the amount of times I have come close to something bad happening."

Q "I feel comfortable walking around campus at all hours of the day."

Q "I have never felt insecure on campus. At night, there are multiple lights on and many security guards around campus."

Q **"Campus police are good, maybe too good**... they sometimes show up when unnecessary. Been there, done that."

Q "I've walked down Bourbon and Canal all alone at midnight on a Friday before, and I've also walked from Quills to JL alone in the same time frame. You want to know what's scarier? The second one. **Walking down an isolated street like Maple can make you feel very nervous.** Since the quarter is always packed, it's less likely for some one to abduct you if you pretend you're apart of one group of people. You can survive in this city alone, but you better watch yourself."

The College Prowler Take On...
Safety & Security

Students all concur that they feel safe while walking on Tulane's grounds, but feel threatened or scared when in the city at night. Theft of bikes, purses, cell phones, and Tulane Student IDs happen on a daily basis, and this is even a form of entertainment in The Hullabaloo's (Tulane's student newspaper) Crime Watch section. The best advice for anyone in New Orleans, especially students, is to stay in groups – this goes double at night. The worst safety threats happen to people walking by themselves, especially in areas outside of the Tulane campus.

The university's police force is made up of 36 full-time officers who are state-certified, as well as around 40 part-time, trained students. They offer many services, such as walking escorts and emergency phones, but these are only available on Tulane campus; once you get into New Orleans itself, you're largely on your own. TUPD is helpful, but seem to give out more parking tickets than warnings about alcohol abuse, for example. Overall, security is definitely a concern around New Orleans, but probably not enough to dissuade potential students. A little bit of common sense goes a long way in making the city a safe place and getting the amazing experience of New Orleans' many cultural districts.

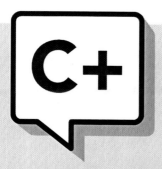

The College Prowler™ Grade on

Safety & Security: C+

A high grade in Safety & Security means that students generally feel safe, campus police are visible, blue light phones and escort services are readily available, and safety precautions are not overly necessary.

Computers

The Lowdown On...
Computers

High-Speed Network?
Yes.

Wireless Network?
Yes. It works everywhere except for some of the older dorms.

Operating Systems:
Windows, MAC, OS and UNIX

Free Software:
Windows: Antivirus software, Adobe Acrobat Reader 6, Eudora 6.01, Meeting Maker 7.1, Netscape Communicator 7.1 , Pop-up Stopper, SSH 3.2.9, Windows patches for Microsoft ASN.1 Library Vulnerabilities, WinZip 8.1, and X-Win32 version 6.0

Macintosh: Virex Anti-Virus Software, Adobe Acrobat Reader, Eudora, MacSFTP, Netscape

Linux: McAfee Virus Scan software updates, Netscape, Adobe Acrobat Reader 5.6

Discounted Software

Windows XP Professional: $60.94

Office XP Professional: $58.28

Office 2003 Professional: $58.28

Mac OS X 10.3 "Panther": $65.00

Office v. X for $55.38

Macromedia Dreamweaver MX: $65.00

24-Hour Labs

Willow Cyber café is open 24 hours a day
(but PJ's closes at 2am)

Charge to Print?

$0.10 black and white pages, $1.00 color pages; each student
has a $25 printing allowance, and printing above that is billed
through a debit of the student ID card

Did You Know?

To see everywhere you can connect to the wireless
network, check out the "Wireless Tulane Project," at
http://www2.tulane.edu/wireless_tulane.cfm.

Cable here is free here thanks to TUCAN. All you
need is a TV with a cable hook-up, and you'll be watching
MTV and Cartoon Network to your heart's content. Since this
is basic cable, however, there's no HBO or Showtime.

Students Speak Out On...
Computers

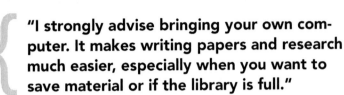

"I strongly advise bringing your own computer. It makes writing papers and research much easier, especially when you want to save material or if the library is full."

Q **"I've definitely benefited from having my own laptop;** most people I know have one. It's the best way to go to stay on top of things on Blackboard, Tulane Webmail, etc."

Q "I have my own computer, and **the network is awesome.** I know nothing about the computer labs."

Q "I don't go to computer labs because I have my own computer. The network is a little slow, but it works. **Tech. Support is very helpful."**

Q **"I always use the library computers.** They rock for checking out internet sites and research stuff. All the computers that I've seen are up-to-date Dell PCs."

Q "I would bring my own computer because **the computer labs can be crowded at certain times,** and it's a pain to wait."

Q **"The computer network works well, with high-speed internet in all rooms.** The labs are sufficient, but you will want your own computer. It is worth mentioning that our wireless network rocks, and works almost anywhere on camps."

Q "I feel paralyzed when the Internet goes down. **I don't know how people manage to go through college without their own computer.**"

Q "The network connection is pretty fast, I don't use the computer labs. **Having your own computer is very convenient.**"

The College Prowler Take On...
Computers

Internet at Tulane is fast and free, there is a large and accessible wireless network, and printing is free (to a point – you get at least 250 pages). While Tulane's computer labs may seem a bit scattered at first, they've complied with student demand in creating **Willow Cyber Café** – a multi-purpose room with computers, space to work, interesting décor, and PJ's Coffee right next door.

You'll want to have your own computer for both convenience and necessity. It's also a good idea – though not quite as important – to get your own printer, because you never know when you will need to print a handout or presentation notes before class. A laptop should definitely be something to consider at Tulane, as well, because of the extensive wireless network that Technology Services has set up across campus. You can connect at almost any of the academic buildings and at the newer residence halls as well. This can be a great asset because it allows you to work anywhere with your own computer.

File-sharing isn't a strong issue at Tulane right now, but these things can change pretty quickly given the legal climate. Sharing copyrighted materials is discouraged by Technology Services, and students are instructed to uninstall any peer-to-peer programs. Tulane's technicians are excellent with helping incoming freshman to set up their internet when they move in, and with fixing computer problems for students throughout the year.

B

The College Prowler™ Grade on

Computers: B

A high grade in Computers designates that computer labs are available, the computer network is easily accessible, and the campus' computing technology is up to date.

Facilities

The Lowdown On...
Facilities

Student Center:
The UC

Athletic Center:
Reily Recreation Center

Libraries:
9

Popular Places to Chill:
Since the construction of the UC started in December of 2003, there isn't really a core meeting place for students. People go to the Pavilion or hang out in PJ's on Willow, mostly.

Campus Size in Acres:
110 acres

What Is There to Do On Campus?

Concerts/Performances:

There's a show every month or so on campus. This year, Guster, The Roots, Outkast, Colin Quinn, and Mitch Hedburg have come to Tulane to perform.

Speakers:

Notable people are constantly coming to Tulane to speak to students about specific fields or majors.

Theater:

The Tulane Theater and Dance department is constantly performing for the community. This spring, they did performances of "A Midsummer Night's Dream", "Richard III", and "Macbeth" for the annual Tulane Shakespeare Festival. There have also been performances of "Agnes of God," "The Fifth of July," and "The Vagina Monologues."

Sports:

Our men and women's basketball teams play in Fogelman Arena, and our baseball team plays home games on campus at Turchin Stadium. You can also watch the tennis matches, soccer games, and other sports on campus. Football games are played either at the Superdome or at Tad Gormley Stadium off campus.

Movie Theatre on Campus?

Movies in McAlister Auditorium: $2.00 with a student ID, $3.00 without. Plays fairly new movies on most Fridays and Saturday nights, usually at 8pm. There is a special performance of The Rocky Horror Picture Show for Halloween, and they host a "TUCP All Nighter" at the end of the 2nd semester. Sources tell us that in years past, they've shown 3D porn.

Bar on Campus?

Students 21 and up can buy beer at the Big Easy Café

Coffeehouse on Campus?

There are 2 PJ's coffee houses on Willow St., in Willow hall and in Percival Stern Hall in the academic quad.

Students Speak Out On...
Facilities

"Some of the facilities are amazing, like the Reily Center and the Business school. Others are HORRIBLE. The freshman dorms and the dance/theater department definitely get the shaft on financing."

"The workout center is amazing, the cafeteria is okay, and the library could use some serious improvement."

"The student center doesn't exist as of now! Reily is amazing. I don't know much about the computer labs."

"Compared to the other schools in the area, the facilities are really nice."

"For the most part, the facilities are good. The dorms are really old and quite disgusting."

"The facilities here are superb. However, with the renovation of the University Center, it has posed a bit of an inconvenience."

"The facilities for athletes, technology, etc. are excellent and the new student center is under construction at the moment"

"I'm at Reily every day. It's the best gym I've ever had a membership to. There are a lot of good classes, like Abs and such, that are free."

Q "Athletic center, aka Reily, is very nice. Facilities are very adequate. Computers are also up-to-date and in good shape. **The Student Center is a circus tent, but in the future that will be better."**

The College Prowler Take On...
Facilities

Back in the good old days, Tulane had a Subway, Pizza Hut, and Chick-Fil-A. That's all gone now because of UC construction. Simply put, the Pavilion – the other main alternative – doesn't cut it, and many students do not like it because of its lack in restaurant choices and the cramped layout of the bookstore. Once the UC construction is complete, there will be a much better place for students to gather on campus; with a January 2006 opening date, however, current and upcoming students are going to have to cope for awhile. In terms of athletic facilities, Reily is an excellent gym with fairly new cardio equipment and a large weight room. There are a lot of fitness classes that you can take for free because of the student membership to the gym, and there are also Yoga, Pilates, and the popular "Shake Down" (pole dancing) classes available for a fee.

Bruff and Howard Tilton, the main libraries, are older and more dated buildings that hopefully will be remodeled in the near future. Some residence halls (especially those for freshmen) and other buildings are also in obvious need of renovations, but the university seems to be continually improving its facilities. Most buildings on campus, especially in the academic quad, are beautiful buildings and go well with the green spaces and the large trees surrounding them.

B+

The College Prowler™ Grade on

Facilities: B+

A high Facilities grade indicates that the campus is aesthetically pleasing and well maintained, facilities are state-of-the-art, and libraries are exceptional. Other determining factors include the quality of both athletic and student centers and an abundance of things to do on campus.

Campus Dining

The Lowdown On...
Campus Dining

Freshman Meal Plan Requirement?

Yes

Meal Plan Average Cost:

$1685

Places to Grab a Bite with Your Meal Plan

Bruff Commons has a salad bar, soup, cereal, a grill, a vegan and vegetarian section, and a desert bar. Many of the hot meals are Cajun dishes (there's a lot of jambalaya, shrimp Creole, and every Monday is red beans and rice day). Every freshman is required to have a meal plan to eat here, so you'll run into a lot of your classmates when you eat.

Open 7am-8:30pm Monday-Thursday, 7am-8pm on Fridays, and 10:30am-8pm on Saturday and Sunday.

→

Big Easy Café has burgers, pizza, a deli, and is the only place on campus to get chicken fingers. Open from 11am-7am (yes, 7 in the morning!) Monday through Sunday.

The Pavilion (The Bubble) has a Taco Bell, Einstein's Brothers Bagels, a sushi bar, Noodle's etc., Far East Fusion, and a Freshens Smoothie Bar. Various restaurants open and close at different times.

The Drawing Board is in the Richardson Memorial (Architecture) building, and has quick deli-style food. Open Mon - Fri: 8am - 6:30pm.

Le Gourmet has wraps and quesadillas. You can get salsa, glass-bottled coke, éclairs, and even pâté here. Open Mon - Thu: 10am - 9pm, Fri: 10am - 8pm, Sat & Sun: 12pm - 6pm

Reily's Freshens' Smoothie Bar makes for a good post-workout reward. It's identical to the one in the Pavilion. Open Mon - Fri: 10am - 8pm, Sat & Sun: 10am - 6pm.

24-Hour On-Campus Eating?

Nothing is open 24/7, but there's always something available. If The Big Easy isn't open, then Bruff or something in the bubble is.

Student Favorites

Le Gourmet

Einstein Brothers' Bagels

Did you know?

Students have the option of putting "Greenbucks" or debit money onto their Tulane cards to eat in the Pavilion. (it's best to go with the debit option, because you can only spend Greenbucks on food and you can't use them for laundry, coffee at PJ's, or at the bookstore – you can with debit). There are also Kosher meal plans available.

Students Speak Out On...
Campus Dining

"There is not much variety on campus and the campus stores offer very little selection. It's also expensive to eat at places other than Bruff. They make is seem like you're getting a good deal, but you aren't."

"**Dining hall does its job**, though it gets old quickly."

"Bruff really is not that great, it gets old real fast; but then again, that is the case with any college. **The Pavilion is great, I am obsessed with Einstein's Bagels.**"

"**Bruff's food is decent but repetitive.**"

"**I avoid eating here** like the black plague."

"**You'll become a vegetarian.** You don't want to eat the meat here. I've nicknamed the tuna "asphalt fish" for obvious reasons. Good things at Bruff: Baked Potato Soup, Grilled Cheese, and they occasionally have 'special days' with themes like carnival or fiesta or formal, and those days they have really good food."

"Food on campus is good, though it can become repetitive. **Late night dining is good at the Big Easy Café** (though the name is quite cheesy). Dining halls are decent and fairly clean."

Q "The food is substantial, but **if you want to eat healthy, your options are very limited.** Better get used to sandwiches!"

Q "The food on campus is decent. **Bruff has its good days and bad days.** The best on-campus establishment is the Drawing Board that's in the Architecture Building."

Q **"The meal plan kinda sucks at times,** but for the first year it's not so bad. I got off it after my freshman year, but hey, it could be much worse."

The College Prowler Take On...
Campus Dining

No one you talk to on campus is going to tell you that Bruff is the best and has really great food. Most will say simply that it is food, and you eat it not because it's good, but because you must eat. For what it's worth, Bruff Commons is all-you-can-eat dining, and the other eateries on campus are set up so that meal dollars (or "Greenbuck$") buy essentially the same things as real cash. However, for the most versatility it's best to choose the "debit" option over the Greenbuck system – you can use the cash you put on your student ID to buy much more than food this way, so it's a lot more convenient (and still safer than carrying cash).

The best thing Bruff has to offer is its breakfast buffet, and occasionally the "theme nights" that have specific types of food, like nachos for Latino night or cotton candy and corn dogs for carnival night. The Big Easy Café opened in March 2004 and replaced the Rat, which was in the UC. It has the same food, but it does not have the same character (like the crack on the glass front door that looked like a bullet hole) and it is not as spacious. There's an Einstein's Bagels and a Taco Bell, but everyone misses the Subway, Pizza Hut, and Chick-Fil-A that existed before. You'll get food delivered or go out to eat a lot, once the splendor of Bruff has worn thin.

The College Prowler™ Grade on
Campus Dining:
C+

Our grade on Campus Dining addresses the quality of both school-owned dining halls and independent on campus restaurants as well as the price, availability, and variety of food available.

Off-Campus Dining

The Lowdown On...
Off-Campus Dining

Restaurant Prowler: Popular Places to Eat!

Pelican Club
Food: Modern Creole-Acadian / International
Address: 312 Exchange Place (in the French Quarter)
New Orleans, Louisiana 70130
Phone: 504-523-5104
Email: info@pelicanclub.com
Cool Features: Classically designed rooms in a large, 19th century French Quarter townhouse, with original contemporary paintings by New Orleans artists. 350 wines are on their extensive wine list. Reservations recommended.
Price: $20-30 for an entrée
Hours: Opens at 5pm, close varies

Emeril's Delmonico
Food: Classic Creole
Address: 1300 St. Charles Ave
New Orleans, LA 70130
Phone: 504.525.4937
Fax: 504.595.2206
Cool Features: Reservations strongly recommended; business casual

→

attire; owned and operated by famous chef Emeril Lagasse

Price: $13-26 for lunch, $20-40 for dinner

Hours: Lunch: Mon-Fri, 11:30a-2:00p; Dinner: Sun-Thu, 6:00p-10:00p and Fri-Sat, 6:00p-11:00p; Brunch Sun, 10:30a-2:00p

Bacco

Food: Italian

Address: 310 Chartres Street New Orleans, Louisiana 70130

Phone: (504) 522-2426

Fax: (504) 521-8323

Cool Features: Dress code is upscale casual; celebrated as one of New Orleans' top romantic restaurants; acclaimed as one of the best restaurants in the city by Zagat and Food and Wine magazine

Price: Lunch entrees are $8-15, dinner between $15-25

Hours: Lunch Daily from 11:30 a.m-2:00 p.m; Dinner Sunday-Thursday 6:30-9:30 p.m., Friday and Saturday 6:00-10:30p.m.

Red Fish Grill

Food: Seafood

Address: 115 Bourbon Street New Orleans, Louisiana 70130

Phone: (504) 598-1200

Cool Features: Casual dress code; on Bourbon Street, but its before you get to the "soul of the street" (i.e.: you can bring small children without worry that they'll see something inappropriate); try the

Chocolate Bread Pudding!

Price: lunch is in the $7 - $12 dollar range, dinner $13 - $22

Hours: Lunch daily 11:00 a.m. - 3:00 p.m.; Dinner nightly 5:00 - 11:00 p.m.

Café Giovanni

Food: Italian

Address: 117 Rue Decatur New Orleans, Louisiana 70130

Phone: (504) 529-2154

Cool Features: Opera singers, great Italian food, and romantic atmosphere makes it the perfect date restaurant.

Price: $20-25

Hours: Daily from 5:30pm-10pm

Zoë Bistro

Food: French

Address: At the W Hotel 333 Poydras Street New Orleans, LA 70130

Phone: (504) 207-5018

Cool Features: Amazing Crème Brule, and there isn't a bad wine on the list; very sophisticated atmosphere.

Price: Starters from $7 to $14; entrées from $6 to $19 at lunch, $16 to $48 at dinner

Copeland's Cheesecake Bistro

Food: Cajun

Address: 2001 St. Charles Avenue New Orleans, LA 70130

Phone: 504-593-9955
Fax: 504-593-9966
Cool Features: Take-out; catering; valet parking; full bar; reservations are recommended.
Price: $15-30
Hours: Mon-Thurs 11 am-11 pm; Fri-Sat 11 am-1 am; Sun 10:30 am-11 pm.

NOLA
Food: Classic Creole
Address: 534 St. Louis Street New Orleans, LA 70130
Phone: 504.522.6652
Fax: 504.524.6178
Cool Features: This is also owned by Emeril; reservations recommended; casual to business attire; has a third-floor private dining rooms for parties of 20-70
Price: Dinner entrées are $30-40, lunch entrees are $15-25
Hours: Lunch: Mon-Sat, 11:30a-2:00p; Dinner: Sun-Thu, 6:00p-10:30p and Fri-Sat, 6:00p-11:00p

Arnaud's
Food: Classic Creole
Address: 813 Bienville St. New Orleans, Louisiana 70112
Phone: 866-230-8892
Fax: 504-581-7908
Cool Features: One of the most famous restaurants in the city; features an oyster bar and live jazz
Price: $20-40 for a dinner entrée
Hours: Lunch Monday through Friday, 11:30 am to 2:30 pm.

Dinner daily from 6 to 10 pm and Friday and Saturday nights 'til 10:30 pm. Sunday Brunch is served from 10:00 am to 2:30 pm

Mike Anderson's
Food: Seafood
Address: 215 Bourbon Street New Orleans, Louisiana 70130
Phone: (504) 524-3884
Address: 1 Poydras Street, Ste 163 (In the Riverwalk Food Court) New Orleans, Louisiana 70130
Phone: (504) 522-7727
Cool Features: The Bourbon Street location has a private room for parties on the second floor, with balcony that looks onto Bourbon Street.
Price: $12-22
Hours: Sunday - Thursday 11:30 am - 10:00 pm, Friday – Saturday 11:30 am - 11:00 pm

Commander's Palace
Food: Creole Seafood
Address: 1403 Washington Avenue New Orleans, LA 70130
Phone: (504) 899-8221
Cool Features: Dress is upscale – jackets preferred at dinner (no shorts).
Price: $30.00-$40.00 per dinner entrée
Hours: Lunch hours: Monday-Friday 11:30am-2:00pm; Dinner hours: Monday-Sunday 6:00pm-10:00pm; Jazz Brunch Saturday 11:30am-1:00pm Sunday 10:30am-1:30pm

Café Du Monde
Food: Dessert Café
Location: French Market,
800 Decatur Street
New Orleans, LA 70116
Open 24 hours
Phone: 504-525-4544

Riverwalk Marketplace,
One Poydras, Suite 27
New Orleans, La, 70130
Open Mon-Sat 8am-9pm;
Sun 8am-7pm
Phone: 504-587-0841

New Orleans Centre,
1400 Poydras, Suite 572
New Orleans, La, 70112
Open Mon-Fri 7am-8pm; Sat
9:30am-8pm; Sun 11:30am-
6pm
Phone: 504-587-0842

Lakeside Mall,
3301 Veterans Blvd
Suite 104, Metairie, La, 70002
Open Mon-Fri 7am-9pm, Sat
8am-9pm, Sun 11am-6pm
Phone: 504-834-8694
Cool Features: Home of the
world famous beignets and
coffee; the one in the French
Market has a very large patio,
and is a good way to take a
break when shopping. They
only take cash!
Price: About $5.00 for an order
of beignets and a Café Au Lait

Fresco's
Food: Sandwiches, Pizza
Address: 7625 Maple St.
New Orleans, LA 70118
Phone: 504.862.6363
Cool Features: Delivery until
3am; good student specials
Price: $10-15
Hours: Daily 11:30am-3am

O'Henrys
Food: American
Address: 634 South Carrollton
Avenue
New Orleans, LA 70118
Phone: 504-866-9741
Fax: 504-866-0008
Cool Features: Full bar on
site; free peanuts, and you can
throw the shells on the floor
Price: About $10 per entrée
Hours: Monday-Thursday and
Sunday 11am-12am; Friday-
Saturday 11am-1am

Best Pizza:
Papa John's

Best Mexican:
Superior Grille

Best Breakfast:
House of Blue's Jazz Brunch
(more so for the atmosphere)

Best Healthy
Fresco's

Best Wings:
Wing Zone

Best Place To Take Your Parents

Pelican Club

Closest Grocery Stores:

Winn Dixie

500 North Carrollton Avenue,
New Orleans, LA 70119

2841 South Claiborne Avenue,
New Orleans, LA 70125

Whole Foods Market

3135 Esplanade Avenue, New
Orleans, LA 70119

Sav-A-Center

400 North Carrollton Avenue,
New Orleans, LA 70119

Did You Know?

New Orleans is the home to authentic Cajun and
Creole food. Chefs use an abundance of seafood,
and especially crawfish, rice, and spices in their
dishes.

Students Speak Out On...
Off-Campus Dining

"Makes you go home and slap your mama! (just kidding!) But seriously, Clancy's, Jacques-Imo's, Emril's, Indigo, Bayona, August Good Friends, Basil Leaf, Equator... I could go on forever!!"

Q "You can find **tons of great variety off campus,** from super expensive (Delmonico's) to totally reasonable (Slim Goodies Diner)."

Q **"The food off campus is incredible!** There are so many choices. Plus, you have the New Orleans food culture on top of all your normal American restaurants."

Q "There are **awesome restaurants within walking/streetcar distance.** Any restaurant on Maple Street like Fresco's, Bravo's, and Houston's on St. Charles rock!"

Q **"New Orleans has some of the most amazing restaurants in the country!"**

Q "Food off campus is very good. **Cheesecake Bistro and Frescos are excellent."**

Q **"Restaurants in New Orleans are amazing.** My favorite spots include Mona's Café, The Garlic Clove, Dunbar's, and Café Freret."

Q "I love the food here, but **I miss real Mexican food.** Don't go to Vera Cruz!! If anything, Superior Grill is the best spot I've been to."

Q "Local food is okay. **The best place is in walking distance is The Camille Grille.**"

Q **"Restaurants off campus are filled with the best food you can find anywhere.** Each restaurant has some signature specialty like white chocolate bread pudding or sweet cornbread."

The College Prowler Take On...
Off-Campus Dining

This is Emril's country, and with that comes great restaurants. People come here from all over the U.S. to taste the one-of-a-kind Cajun cooking in New Orleans. If you're not into all the spice that Cajun food is famous for, the city has nationally acclaimed and prize winning Italian and seafood restaurants as well. Café Giovanni, an Italian restaurant in the Quarter, is a great example. The Chinese and Mexican food here is not great, but there are a few places that are worth visiting. Pretty much all Chinese takeout is the same, but some places are a lot cheaper than others.

Unlike a lot of cities in the States, there are dozens of excellent restaurants within neighborhoods that are away from the tourist-driven French Quarter and Market. When students want to go out to eat on a school night and don't want to go all the way downtown, there are plenty of places within walking distance, such as Frescos, O'Henrys, and the Camilla Grill, or a short streetcar ride away like the Cheesecake Bistro, Copeland's, Superior Grille, Houston's, and Voodoo BBQ, among others. There are many small cafés and restaurants down Maple and Oak Street and all through the Uptown area that are relatively inexpensive and have a unique atmosphere. New Orleans is home to some of the best food in the country, and definitely the best in the South. Bon Appétit!

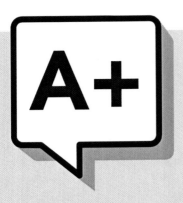

The College Prowler™ Grade on

Off-Campus Dining: A+

"A high off campus dining grade implies that off campus restaurants are affordable, accessible, and worth visiting. Other factors include the variety of cuisine and the availability of alternative options (vegetarian, vegan, kosher, etc.)"

On-Campus Housing

The Lowdown On...
On-Campus Housing

Room Types:
Single; Double; Super Single; 2, 4, and 8 person suite; 3, 4, and 5 bedroom apartments

Best Dorms:
Aron

Willow

Mayer

Worst Dorms:
Monroe

Sharp

Phelps

Dormitories

**Butler Hall
(The Freshmen Honors Dorm)**
Floors: 8
Total Occupancy: 252
Bathrooms: Community
Co-Ed: Yes
Room Types: Double, Super Singles

Special Features: 7 study lounges; carpeted rooms; two kitchens, three laundry rooms; chests of drawers are built into a study desk that runs the width of the room

Josephine-Louise Hall (or JL: The All-Girl Dorm)

Floors: 3

Total Occupancy: 207

Bathrooms: Community

Co-Ed: No (Female only)

Room Types: Single, Double, and Super Singles

Special Features: Moveable Shaker-style wooden furniture; casement windows and high ceilings; extra-long mattresses; mounted bookshelves; carpeted rooms; cable TV and Internet access; many rooms have a sink and mirror in one corner. This hall has open visitation with a Desk Service Coordinator who is on duty 24 hours a day. All visitors must check their IDs at the desk from 8 p.m. to 8 a.m. Male visitors in the building must be escorted at all times.

Irby (Upperclassmen Dorm)

Floors: 4

Total Occupancy: 210

Bathrooms: Suite-shared

Co-Ed: Yes

Room Types: Suite-style halls that have four rooms sharing a bathroom, and there are a limited number of double rooms with a private bath.

Special Features: Kitchen facilities; common areas; study lounges; carpeted rooms; moveable furniture

Mayer (Upperclassmen Dorm)

Floors: 4

Total Occupancy: 248

Bathrooms: Two singles or two doubles share a bathroom

Co-Ed: Yes

Room Types: Singles and Doubles

Special Features: Some rooms have transom windows while others have semi-shared balconies; custom-built movable hardwood furniture is furnished in every room; has cable TV and internet access; carpeted rooms; many social lounges, kitchens, and study lounges. Mayer has two upstairs patios, two top-floor sundecks, and is attached to Le Gourmet.

Monroe (Co-ed Freshman Dorm)

Floors: 12

Total Occupancy: 440

Bathrooms: Community

Co-Ed: Yes, but by wing

Room Types: Mostly double; some single, 6 person suites, and super single

Special Features: Each room has standard twin beds with stationary bolster cabinets above; carpeted rooms; built-in desks, and a chest of drawers located in the closets. Monroe is equipped with a wide range of study lounges, TV rooms, and kitchen facilities.

Willow Residences
(Upperclassmen Dorm)

Floors: Made of 4 buildings (Willow A, B, C, and Leadership Village)

Total Occupancy: 318

Bathrooms: Shared between rooms or suites

Co-Ed: Yes

Room Types: 2 and 4 person suite, super single, loft doubles (Leadership Village only)

Special Features: In A, B, and C, each floor has its own social lounge, kitchen and study rooms; in A there is a seminar room, a large multipurpose lounge, and a PJ's coffee; in The Leadership Village, 20 students live in single-room suites, and 40 students live in two-story loft double room suites – the lofts have spiral staircases and third-story balconies. Students have to apply to get into Leadership Village.

Warren
(The Other All-Girl Dorm)

Floors: 3

Total Occupancy: 148

Bathrooms: Community; some suite-shared

Co-Ed: No

Room Types: Double, Single, Super single, some 4 person suites

Special Features: The main floor has a spacious lounge, several study rooms for individual work or group meetings, and a computer lab; the building has a second floor balcony and a roof-top sunning porch.

Patterson Hall
(The Substance-Free Living Dorm)

Floors: 3

Total Occupancy: 116

Bathrooms: Some community, some suite-shared, some doubles with private baths.

Co-Ed: Yes, by floor or by suite

Room Types: 4-person Suite, Double Rooms, Super Single

Special Features: This is a substance-free dorm. There is moveable Shaker-style wooden furniture and extra-long twin beds in each room; the first floor has a large common room that features a pool table, large-screen TV, a laundry room, a kitchen, and study room; there's a computer lab on the second floor and a large study room on the third.

Phelps Hall (Upperclassmen (with some freshmen) Dorm)

Floors: 4

Total Occupancy: 210

Bathrooms: four rooms sharing a spacious bathroom, or double room with private bath

Co-Ed: Yes, by suite

Room Types: 2 and 8 Person suites; super single

Special Features: All rooms are double occupancy with large picture windows; furniture is moveable; cable TV and Internet access; study lounges and kitchen facilities; wraparound balconies.

Aron Residences (Upperclassmen Apartments)

Floors: 3
Total Occupancy: 493
Bathrooms: 2 bathrooms per apartment
Co-Ed: Yes
Room Types: Aron consists of three, four, and five bedroom apartments which all are completely furnished.
Special Features: Each apartment has central heat/air conditioning, closet organizers, cable TV and Internet access, local phone connection, and all-electric kitchen appliances including dishwashers. The Aron/Willow office has vacuum cleaners, games and movies available for checkout. There is a laundry facility, a social lounge, and several outdoor grills. Electricity is billed separately and not included in the room charge. The mandatory $300 commitment deposit becomes an electric deposit, and monthly electric charges are taken out of this deposit.

Sharp
(Co-ed Freshman Dorm)

Floors: Sharp is L-shaped, with seven floors on one wing and four on the other wing.
Total Occupancy: 456
Bathrooms: Community
Co-Ed: Yes
Room Types: double, single, super single
Special Features: Laundry facilities; pool table, large screen TV, and front desk; rooms have standard twin beds with stationary bolster cabinets and chests of drawers in the closets; study lamps above the desks; cable TV hook-up and internet access; study lounges located throughout the hall.

Undergrads On Campus:
55%

Number of Dormitories:
12

Number of University-Owned Apartments:
1

Percentage of Students in Singles:
8%

Percentage of Students in Doubles:
71%

Percentage of Students in Triples/ Suites:
1%

Percentage of Students in Apartments:
20%

Bed Type
Depends – some have extra long twin, other have twin beds, and Leadership Village has lofts

Available for Rent
Micro-fridges

Cleaning Service?
Yes – JaniKing, the cleaning service on campus, cleans the community bathrooms daily and the suite bathrooms every other day.

What You Get
All dorms have carpeted rooms, cable TV/Internet/telephone hookup, kitchen facilities, common areas, and air conditioning

Did You Know?

The dorms New Doris and Zemurray were destroyed in 2003 and 2004, and are now being constructed into new co-ed freshman dorms for future classes. After that construction, there will be 7 dorms for freshman on campus (still 5 for upperclassmen)

Students Speak Out On...
On-Campus Housing

"Monroe should be torn down or condemned! I don't even know if there are actually nice dorms, but I think that most of the rest are tolerable. I will give Monroe credit for having a good view from the higher rooms!"

Q "HRL confuses me. They paint the white walls of my hallway white again in the middle of the week when that money could be better placed in replacing our moldy shower curtains, for example. There are moments when the heat/AC doesn't work, and they're constantly fixing our water, so we'll go a day without it. Now, don't get the impression that this place is a hellhole. Go look at UT-Austin's dorms and then you'll think that Tulane has the best dorms you'll ever see. Simply put, **they're better than a lot of schools, but when it comes to private schools, they suck.**"

Q "JL, Warren, and Phelps are very nice dorms. However, **Sharp and Monroe are the center of freshman life.** It's a give-take situation."

Q **"The dorms are gross but so much fun.** A totally perfect college experience. I would avoid the all-girl dorms (JL and Warren) and the honors dorm (Butler)."

Q "Sharp and Monroe are the 2 major freshman dorms (co-ed), and Sharp is slightly nicer. **For girls, the all-girls dorm JL is very nice.**"

Q **"The dorms are crap.** I can't believe that I have to pay to live in them. The bathrooms are disgusting and the rooms are not soundproof at all. To prove my point, there was puke outside my room (in Butler) for 2 weeks before it was cleaned up, and when they did clean it, it was 1 in the morning"

Q "I think the dorms are fairly typical. The dorms to avoid are Monroe and Sharp. JL and Warren are nice for women, and **New Doris is the only freshman dorm with suite-style rooms."**

Q "It depends on what you want. Sharp and Monroe are the old freshman dorms. They're kind of decrepit, but they're also the most social. **Butler is the honors dorm – nice if you want to study."**

Q **"Freshman dorms stink, but the upper-class ones are good.** Willow and Monroe are great. Housing is only guaranteed freshman year (which sucks.)"

Q **"Housing is like a prison cell**, not reflective of the price."

Q "The dorms are decent with the exception of Monroe and Sharp. **Aron Residences and Willow are the desired dorms** on campus. However, many people opt for off-campus housing."

The College Prowler Take On...
On-Campus Housing

Students have few good words to say about Monroe and Sharp. They are old, ugly, and pretty gross, but there's a big social factor about living in these 2 dorms. JL and Warren are nice all-girls dorms; they're quiet and most of the rooms have sinks in them, but they're usually less social than the co-ed dorms and you have to go out of your way to meet boys. For upperclassmen, Irby and Phelps are the two dorms that people hate the most. These looks like motels because the doors to the rooms face outside, and they are older buildings. Students tend to prefer Willow, Mayer, and Aron, but mostly juniors and seniors get intoAron and Willow. Butler, the honors dorm, is old and ugly, but is in a great spot (across the street from Bruff and a block away from Reily). Patterson is a good choice and is nicer than Irby, Phelps, Sharp, or Monroe; however, it's a substance-free living environment, which is a bad thing to many students that live on campus. 2 new dorms are being constructed, but there's still very little room for the students who want to live on campus. You are guaranteed housing only for freshman year, so don't be surprised if you get waitlisted for housing your sophomore and junior year (for 2004-2005, there were more than 500 people on the housing waitlist!). Tulane students largely think the dorms are gross, but livable.

The College Prowler™ Grade on
Campus Housing: C

A high Campus Housing grade indicates that dorms are clean, well-maintained and spacious. Other determining factors include variety of dorms, proximity to classes and social atmosphere.

Off-Campus Housing

The Lowdown On...
Off-Campus Housing

Undergrads in Off-Campus Housing:
56%

Average Rent for a Studio Apartment:
$650 per month

Average Rent for a One-Bedroom Apartment:
$500-700 per month

Average Rent for a Two-Bedroom Apartment:
$800-1000 per month

Popular Areas:
Uptown
Small streets off Broadway
Napoleon Ave.,
in between Louisiana Ave. and Constantinople St.

For Assistance Contact:
http://www2.tulane.edu/och/och/

Students Speak Out On...
Off-Campus Housing

"Off campus housing is cheap and available if you're interested. I'm living off campus next year for cheaper than it would be to stay on campus, and I've got a really prime location next to a fraternity house."

Q "Pretty convenient and pretty cheap. **People typically live in houses that are split up into "apartments.** I lived in a gorgeous 3 bedroom that was about 2 feet from campus for my last 2 years. It's nice to get that personal space again, but I think I could have been happy staying on campus as well."

Q **"It is not especially convenient,** but once you've been there for awhile it'll be easier because you'll have people you know with apartments to give up."

Q "New Orleans is an old city full of old houses. **Off campus housing is expensive in any big city,** and if you're going to opt for it you'll have to find some friends to join you in paying the rent."

Q "There are lots of options for housing off campus. There aren't a lot of apartment complexes around, but there are a lot of houses where you can rent out the basement or half the house or the whole house. **It isn't very expensive either."**

Q "If you're going to look for a place, **stay in Uptown, or look in Metairie.** There are some really shady places in New Orleans, and living in them is very unsafe."

Q "If you're worried about security, **there are plenty of apartment complexes that are gated.** Mine even has a pool and a gym, so it's really nice."

The College Prowler Take On...
Off-Campus Housing

Living on campus can be fun for the first few semesters, but after your sophomore year you'll want to get your own place. Students tend to rent out houses with 3, 4, or even 5 of their closest friends and split the rent, rather than getting their own apartment.

You might think to disregard this section because you know you will never have a car during college, thus making it impossible for you to have you own place off campus. However, the reality is most students live within a mile of Tulane, so many walk or bike to campus each day (which makes things a lot easier, because parking is a nightmare). Many upperclassmen have houses on the small side streets that branch off of Broadway, the street predominately occupied by fraternity and sorority houses. Very few stray from Uptown because neighborhoods in the surrounding area are poor and filled with crime.

It's best to ask around with older classmates if an area has been crime-free in years past before moving in. It can be pretty dangerous, so it's best to be careful.

The farthest students will live is in Metairie, a glorified suburb that's about 20 to 30 minutes away from campus. Metairie does have its advantages, with its giant Target, a commercial movie theater, and all that suburbia has to offer. However, the traffic tends to build up during rush hour, and the drive can get tedious to make every day.

There's more responsibility with having your own place, and it seems harder to get up in the morning for 9AM classes when you live off campus than when you lived on campus in a building that was 30 steps away from your classroom. However, the incentives of having all out parties and even owning a pet make off campus housing the way to go for the upperclassmen years.

The College Prowler™ Grade on

Off-Campus Housing: A

A high grade in Off-Campus Housing indicates that apartments are of high quality, close to campus, affordable, and easy to secure.

Diversity

The Lowdown On...
Diversity

American Indian:
0.47%

Asian or Pacific Islander:
5.45%

African American:
9.85%

Hispanic:
3.88

White:
79.55%

International:
2.65%

Out of State:
64.62%

Most Popular Religions:

Catholic
Protestant (Baptist, Methodist, Presbyterian)
Jewish

Muslim

Political Activity

On average, Tulane is an apathetic campus. However, there is a large following with the College Republicans and Democrats, and the USG (Undergraduate Student Government) is taken seriously. If you're into politics, there are a lot of groups you can get involved with. The Newspaper, the Tulane Hullabaloo, is pretty liberal – especially the magazine The Arcade that comes out every other week. The Hullabaloo always devotes space to cover the weekly USG meeting, and has had articles about local and national politics. Tulane is mostly liberal, but if you are a Conservative you'll definitely find a big niche of your own.

Gay Tolerance

MOSAIC is a gay-straight alliance club, and the dominant group on campus for promoting tolerance based on sexual orientation. New Orleans and Tulane are both fairly liberal climates, so sexuality isn't a broad problem on campus.

Economic Status

You cannot go to school here without a scholarship and not be rich. With tuition and room and board costing around $40,000 a year, Tulane is extremely expensive. However, a lot of students here are here on scholarship, so there is a certain population of middle and lower class students.

Minority Clubs

African-American Congress of Tulane, Asian American Students United, Celtic Society, Indian Association of Tulane University, International Student Association of Tulane, Latin and American Student Association, Mexican Students of Tulane ,Middle Eastern Student Association, Multicultural Council, Muslim Educational and Cultural Committee for Awareness, Muslim Student Association, Students Organized Against Racism (SOAR), Tulane African Student Association, Tulane Chinese Student Association (ROC), Tulane Chinese Students & Scholars Association(PRC), Tulane University Celtic Society, Tulane University Vietnamese Association, and Turkish Student Organization

Students Speak Out On...
Diversity

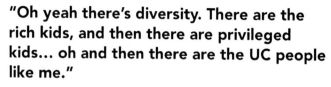

"Oh yeah there's diversity. There are the rich kids, and then there are privileged kids... oh and then there are the UC people like me."

Q "Tulane's **campus is extremely diverse.**"

Q "It's **somewhat diverse, better than most state schools.**"

Q "I find **it has spurts of diversi**ty, but a lot of the same kind of people."

Q "Tulane is **not very diverse at all, unless you are talking in terms of diverse parts of the country.** Most of my classes are not ethnically diverse, and in general the campus isn't either."

Q "A lot of the literature may say it's diverse, but **it's generally made up of a lot of well-off white kids from New York or New Jersey.** It's nothing that takes away from the campus and there are multicultural organizations, but if you're looking for a melting pot of a campus then Tulane isn't exactly that."

Q "Although Tulane tries to portray itself as a diverse university, the majority of the students are upper-class white guys and girls. **There are a lot of students that come from countries all over the world too.**"

Q "Tulane isn't very diverse. **There are mostly Anglo-Saxon/white people.**"

Q "NO. Not even a question."

Q "It's slightly diverse. **It's mostly middle to upper class white Catholics and Jewish people.**"

The College Prowler Take On...
Diversity

Does Tulane have a lot of diversity? The way you answer this question all depends on your past experiences. Naturally, if you went to an elitist private academy with less than a handful of minorities enrolled, you'll get here and see a couple of African Americans and Indian students and will be amazed at the amount of diversity. However, if you went to an inner city high school or a public high school where the white population was slowly becoming a minority, you'll come to Tulane and think this is the largest white population at a school you've seen in a long time. After all, the white population is 80% of the total.

Racially and ethnically, this school is lacking on diversity. There are a lot of strongly represented cultural organizations, but the numbers are small. IATU, Hillel, and the Catholic Center constantly advertise activities that their clubs are putting on each week; joining these groups, or at least going to one activity, will help you better understand different cultures and religions. It's also a good way to meet new people in the fall semester.

The diversity of Tulane comes from the amount of kids hailing from all over the country. You'll have friends that live in California and Manhattan, and that in itself is somewhat diverse. Outside of the Tulane bubble, there is a city that is full of diversity and culture. New Orleans is predominantly African American, and there is also a notable population of Caucasians, Cajuns, and Creoles, among others. It is a type of diversity that is only found in this part of the country, and in a sense, city itself makes up for Tulane's lack of diversity.

The College Prowler™ Grade on

Diversity: D+

A high grade in Diversity indicates that ethnic minorities and international students have a notable presence on campus, and that students of different economic backgrounds, religious beliefs, and sexual preferences are well-represented.

Guys & Girls

The Lowdown On...
Guys & Girls

Men Undergrads:
47%

Women Undergrads:
53%

Birth Control Available?
ECP, Depo-Provera injections, and birth control pills are available by prescription in the women's clinic. Condoms are also available in the men's heath clinic.

Most Prevalent STDs on Campus:
HPV (Genital Warts) is the most common (50% of students tested have this), followed by Chlamydia (10%) and Genital Herpes (8%)

Social Scene:

People love to drink here, so a lot of the social scene revolves around one of the many bars near campus. Students attend frat parties in the fall in order to meet new people. However, there are a lot of groups that are into music and go to concerts, and there are some people that are into art or politics and do things with their group of friends. Basically, your social scene revolves around what group of people you hang out with most, so where you go on a Friday night depends on what the group is doing.

Hookups or Relationships?

Both. A lot of hookups happen all year 'round, but a lot of people have boyfriends/girlfriends that go to different schools, and there are a lot of relationships on campus as well. (A word of advice: you just read that 33% of people have an STD – this is above the national average, and a good thing to keep in mind)

Best Place to Meet Guys/Girls:

You'll be on people-overload during Orientation – you'll meet many people, but you won't remember half the names. Students usually meet the most guys/girls through the dorms or in classes. You'll meet a lot of people at parties, but your closest friends will most likely be through the organizations you join and the people in your hallway. You'll become really good friends with the people who are in your major once you declare one, because you will all be in the same classes together.

Top Places to Hookup:

1. Happy Hour at the Boot on Friday Nights (ends at 9pm)
2. Frat Houses
3. French Quarter
4. TJ Quills

Top Three Places to Find Hotties:

1. The Boot (on Fridays, before 9pm or after 2am)
2. PJ's
3. Reily

Dress Code

A lot of girls dress up practically every day, and it's an unstated rule that the official Tulane shoe is the flip flop. The bookstore sells Tulane flip flops, and guys and girls alike own a pair or two (I personally just bought some, and they are very comfortable). A lot of girls carry around big tote bags as backpacks, and are constantly seen talking on a cell phone or smoking a cigarette.

The average straight college guy has a pretty bland collection of clothes, and they all dress the same. There are a lot of gay and metro-sexual guys at Tulane, so you'll often see a guy walking down McAlister with shoes on that you wish you owned. It's also cool to wear your collar flipped up, and Abercrombie is really popular with the preppy kids.

Then there are kids like myself. On a regular day, I come to class in jeans and a hoodie with my hair everywhere. I like to think that I am a part of the 50% of people who blatantly don't care about their appearance, but a lot do. So if you're looking for a girl/guy, I'd suggest going the extra mile when getting ready, because there's a lot of competition.

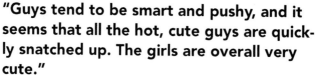

Students Speak Out On...
Guys & Girls

{ **"Guys tend to be smart and pushy, and it seems that all the hot, cute guys are quickly snatched up. The girls are overall very cute."**

"Not the most attractive student body. Some girls are more ritzy than others. A majority I would say are pretty laid back with image… that may not be right. Put it this way, I'm not concerned about looking good every day, and there's no pressure to, so it's nice."

"Most of the guys are hot… until you get to know them."

"Like anywhere else, there are nice people as well as jerks. **The guys are not hot, but there is a small population of hotties.** Most of the girls look anorexic."

"The freshman chicks are hot! They have some good looking ladies here, but the fashion is strange."

"Every now and then you'll find an interesting, smart, good looking guy. But in general, the combination is scarce. **Most of the girls are spoiled rich kids with way too many clothes and too much free time."**

"People here are alright. **There's a percentage of hot girls."**

"Who defines hot? **Many people who attend this school come from similar, suburban, rich backgrounds."**

Q "The girls, in my opinion, are nothing special. Many are rich snobby girls from cities and who don't have much of a brain, but there are definitely exceptions. **I have met a lot of cool girls here as well.**"

Q **"There are some hot guys, not a whole lot.** A lot of them seem to be rather stuck up, but you can find some nice ones. The girls for the most part are cool, a lot of them are very sorority-ish (into dressing up, tanning, etc), but there are plenty who aren't."

The College Prowler Take On...
Guys & Girls

Tulane is not an ugly campus by any means, but there is a minority of really radiantly hot babes. Most guys look average and have an average wardrobe – the most attractive men on campus are gay. The girls tend to dress up more than at your average college campus, and put a lot put effort into their appearance. There a lot of "cool and interesting people" to meet, and a lot like to have a good time along with studying and being typical, intellectual college students.

There are more hookups than actual committed relationships, but you'll find a lot of people with significant others that live elsewhere. Because of the mild weather, you'll see girls sunbathing in practically every month of the year, and people tend to wear tank tops and shorts for the majority of the spring and part of the fall semester. The men of Tulane say that the Newcomb women are the most attractive on campus, and some even have "I love Newcomb Girls" T-Shirts. If you don't love someone for their looks, you'll love them for their intelligence or personality because a lot of the good finds here are the really smart ones. There's not an abundance of nerdy kids or really preppy kids – you see a lot of everything. No matter your type is, you'll find something that you like at Tulane.

B-

The College Prowler™ Grade on
Guys: B-

A high grade for Guys indicates that the male population on campus is attractive, smart, friendly, and engaging, and that the school has a decent ratio of guys to girls.

B+

The College Prowler™ Grade on
Girls: B+

A high grade for Girls not only implies that the women on campus are attractive, smart, friendly, and engaging, but also that there is a fair ratio of girls to guys.

Athletics

The Lowdown On...
Athletics

Athletic Division:
Division I

Conference:

C-USA

Men's Varsity Sports:
Baseball
Basketball
Cross Country,
Football
Golf
Tennis
Track

**Women's
Varsity Sports:**
Basketball
Volleyball
Soccer
Cross Country
Track
Golf
Tennis
Swimming and Diving

Club Sports:
Ballroom Dancing

Baseball

Capoeira

Cricket
Dodge Ball
Fencing
Field Hockey
Gymnastics
Ice Hockey
Judo
Karate
Men's and Women's Lacrosse
Martial Arts
Rock Climbing
Rowing
Rugby
Running
Sailing
Men and Women Soccer
Swimming
Tennis
Ultimate Frisbee
Volleyball
Water Polo
Waterskiing
Wrestling

Basketball
Softball
Ping Pong
Basketball
(these vary every year)

Number of Males Playing Varsity Sports:
172

% of Males Playing Varsity Sports:
3%

Number of Females Playing Varsity Sports:
102

% of Females Playing Varsity Sports:
2%

Intramurals:
Flag Football
Indoor and Outdoor Soccer
Volleyball
Dodge ball
Racquetball Tournaments,
the annual "McAlister Mile"
Biathlon
3-on-3 basketball

Athletic Fields

Tad Gormley Stadium and The Superdome
Football

Fogelman Arena
Basketball

Turchin Stadium, Zephyr Field
 Baseball

Goldring Tennis Stadium
Tennis

George G. 'Sunny' Westfeldt, Jr. Facility
Soccer, Club sports

Brown, Newcomb, UC Quads
 Intramural sports/Club sport practices

School Mascot
Riptide the Pelican, Green Wave

Getting Tickets
Tickets are free to students, and very easy to get

Most Popular Sports
Football is probably the most popular sport on campus, followed by men's basketball.

Best Place to Take a Walk
Audubon Park

Gyms/Facilities

The Wilson Center

This building has all the athletic offices, the Green Wave's weight room and training room, the Mickey Retif Clubhouse, and the Tulane Athletic Hall of Fame Room. You'll also find the Academic Student Services Office and a computer lab here.

Henry Frnka Weight Room

More than 5,000 square feet of training space, and over 30,000 pounds of weights and equipment, as well as medicine balls, hurdles, and other speed/agility equipment. The facility also has video equipment to "evaluate each player to ensure that they exercise properly, effectively and safely," and a surround-sound stereo system.

Reily Student Recreation Center

Houses 150,000 square feet of activity space, including basketball and volleyball courts, racquetball, squash, and (outdoor) tennis courts, a huge weight room and swimming pool, and an elevated indoor track. There are also aerobics rooms, a spinning room, a cardio area, and ping pong tables, as well as new locker rooms complete with saunas and a sun deck. After working out, check out the smoothie bar!

Students Speak Out On...
Athletics

"**Varsity sports are not a big deal, but lots of people get involved in intramural sports and, during the school year, the quads are usually busy with soccer and softball games.**"

Q "**Varsity sports have little momentum**, but some students show up to the games. People participate in IM sports, but it's not huge."

Q "Varsity and IM **sports are as big as you make them**. A lot of people get really into it, but if you're not, it doesn't matter."

Q "They are mediocre. **Our football team sucks, but the baseball team is pretty strong.**"

Q "Sports get less support from students than other colleges. **There are a lot of intramural sports.**"

Q "**Varsity sports are not so good, and IM sports are probably worse.**"

Q "**Do we have a team?**"

Q "**Girls basketball and baseball are the biggest sports on campus, and they receive the most publicity.** IMs are a big part of campus life because it is such a nice break from the stress of class."

Q **"Club sports are the best way to go.** They're more organized then IMs, but less intense than Varsity. I've met some of my closest friends through playing club sports."

The College Prowler Take On...
Athletics

Tulane's athletics department almost got shut down a few years ago, so that gives you an idea of how widely supported and successful the teams are. The baseball and women's basketball teams are some of the best in their divisions, but never have won a championship. Some of the university's baseball and football games are played in the Superdome, the stadium for the city's football team (the Saints), and there is usually a good showing for games that are held there.

A lot of students are involved in club sports because of there are so many more sports offered in club than varsity, and they are much more laid back. Intramurals are fun to participate in, but these tend to be much less organized, and they do not last very long – there are only a few games in a season. Both club and intramural sports are a great way to meet new people, but participation isn't necessary for your social standing. Students who are not involved in sports usually show no support for them or interest in them. No one comes to Tulane because of the sports atmosphere, so if you're a big football or baseball fan, don't be surprised when there isn't a huge following.

B-

The College Prowler™ Grade on
Athletics: B-

A high grade in athletics indicates that students have school spirit, that sports programs are respected, that games are well-attended, and that intramurals are a prominent part of student life.

Nightlife

The Lowdown On...
Nightlife

Club Prowler: Popular Nightlife Spots!

Club 360

World Trade Center, 33rd Floor
2 Canal Street
Phone: (504) 595-8500

This posh, circular club sits atop of New Orleans' World Trade Center. With an all-glass exterior and rotating outer circle, it gives club goers an excellent view of the city as they sip expensive cocktails. The inner circle of the club is for dancing, as DJs play the latest styles from hip-hop to jazz.

Specials: Daylight (beginning at 11am on weekdays, noon on weekends): 1 drink minimum, plays New Orleans jazz, blues

Happy Hour: 4-8pm, $2 off all drinks, $1 drafts and $3 well cocktails

Monday and Wednesday Nights: No cover, 21 and up only; plays acid jazz and chill-out music

Thursday Nights: "Juicy," $10 cover; ladies need to be 18 and up, guys 21 and up; hip hop and pop music

Friday Nights: "Trust," $10 cover; ladies need to be 18 and up, guys 21 and up; $3 Skyy and Jim Bean Black Label Cocktails; DJs play acid jazz and downtempo house

Saturday Night: "Saturday Night Heaven," $10 Cover; 21 and up to get in; DJs play house, trance, breaks, and club music

Sunday Night: "Cosmopolitan Sundays," cover starts at $10; 21 and up to get in; DJs play hip-hop, R&B, reggae, and dance hall music

Cat's Meow

701 Bourbon Street

(504) 523-2788

Considered to be one of the best karaoke bars in the world, The Cat's Meow is a very popular spot on Bourbon for tourists and celebrities alike. Paying the cover charge allows you to sing songs for free, but there can be a long wait, and drinks are a bit on the pricy side. DJs play a wide variety of music in between performances. This place is a guaranteed good time if you go with a group of friends. From 4pm-8pm on weekdays and 2pm-8pm weekends is 3 for 1 Happy Hour

Funky Butt

714 North Rampart Street

(504) 558-0872

A laid back club that's a couple of streets down from Bourbon, The Funky Butt is a prime spot for good jazz and great Creole food. It serves as a restaurant, and local and famous bands come through during all times off the year to play for small audiences. The kitchen is open every night 7pm - 2am, and shows usually start at 10pm.

The House of Blues (HOB)

225 Decatur St.

(504) 529-2624

It's hard to place the HOB into one category. It's a restaurant, club, and concert venue all in one. There's a voodoo garden next to the restaurant and bar that visitors can sit in and chat before a show. The Music Hall events include performances from a number of local, national and international acts 365 days a year; late-night dance parties; and the famous Sunday Gospel Brunch. The Parish is a 5,000 square foot multi-use special event space with a state-of-the-art sound system. There is also a private club called the Foundation Room that is for VIPs and HOB members. There's a prayer room, a dining room, and a lounge that can be used for private parties or for guests during concerts.

OZ

800 Bourbon Street

(504) 593-9491

OZ is considered to be the best gay bar in the French Quarter. It's a great place to go with a couple of friends to dance because the DJs play the latest club music. Happy hour (2 for 1 domestic beer and well drinks) is Monday-Friday from 4pm-10pm, and Saturday and Sunday 4pm-8pm. Fridays are Student Nights, where the cover is free when you bring your student ID.

Club 735

735 Bourbon Street
(504) 581-6742

The ground floor of Club 735 is a smoke-filled raver's paradise that features internationally known DJs. There's also the second-floor Loft, the plush Red Room video lounge, and the balcony which looks out onto Bourbon Street. Madonna even filmed her 'American Pie' video here.

Tuesday Nights: Movie Night, free popcorn; $5 pitchers and $1.50 beer

Thursday Nights: "1984," $1 Rolling Rock all night

Friday and Saturday: No cover until 11pm

Sunday: "Praise" – no cover all night

Bar Prowler:

Tulane students love their bars, and most go to ones around campus. Most are friendly and serve anyone who can get through the door.

The Boot

1039 Broadway St.

(504) 866-9008

By the end of your 1st week at Tulane, you'll know where and what The Boot is. It's a popular place to "pre-game" it before a big party or to meet up with everyone after a night on the town. The Boot serves as the Tulane/Loyola hangout spot for undergrads of all ages. The DJ plays loud but classic songs, and there are multiple TV screens that show sports and news. Fridays is Happy Hour, 4-9pm, with 3 for 1 longnecks.

The Bulldog

3236 Magazine St.

(504) 891-1516

There are no less than 50 beers are on tap at any given time and 250 or so total brands of beer. Also has pool tables, darts, and big screen TVs. This bar is unique in that it gives you the opportunity to try beers from all over the world. This place also has really good bar food. Considered the "best place to drink beer" in 2001 by New Orleans Magazine. Register online at their website (bulldog.draftfreak. com) and get free beer on your birthday. The Bulldog also has the Beer Journey. Complete your card of all 50 draft beers and you get to pick from a lot of cool Bulldog shirts, caps etc. for free and get your name on their plaque of Adventurers.

Mondays: $2 off imports

Tuesday: $1 off import pints

Wednesday: Free pint glass with every pint you buy

Saturday: Wear a Bulldog T-shirt and get $1 off pints until 8pm

Happy Hour: Monday-Thursday 2-7:30, 50 cents off pints, $1 off pitchers, and 2 for 1 mixed drinks

TJ Quills

7620 Maple Street

(504) 866-5205

Also called "Quills" or "TJ's" by students. Not the best bar, but there's no question that you will get served. They have foosball tables, pool, and even through there is no live music the jukebox is constantly playing old favorites and rap music. Open until 2 am Monday-Friday, 3 am on Saturday, and 11 pm on Sunday.

Tuesdays are 25 cent night for beer (you get a small cup, not a longneck).

Other Places to Check Out:

Tiptinas

TwiRopa

F&Ms

Fat Harry's

Bruno's

The Maple Leaf

Coyote Ugly

Dragon's Den

Howl at the Moon

King Pin

N.O. Original Daiquiris

Polynesian Joe's

Spotted Cat

The Dungeon

Three Legged Dog

Whisky Blues

Checkpoint Charlie's

Jimmy's Club

Bars Close At:

Depends on the bar. Some close between 3 and 5AM, and some don't even have a specific closing time

Primary Areas with Nightlife:

French Quarter

Bars around campus

Cheapest Place to Get a Drink:

3 for 1 night Fridays at the Boot

25 cent night at TJ Quill's

Free and open bar when you pay the cover (for ladies 21+) at TriRopa (and other places every once in awhile… check before you go)

Favorite Drinking Games:

Beer Pong

Card Games

Century Club

Quarters

Power Hour

(Movie Title Here) Challenge

- In The Big Lebowski Challenge, for example, you have to drink the same amount of White Russians as Lebowski…

Student Favorites

The Boot, T.J. Quills, F&M's, Bruno's, The House of Blues, The Cat's Meow

Useful Resources for Nightlife

www.nola.com

The Gambit Weekly (a magazine that can be picked up at PJ's),

The Arcade (The Hullabaloo's magazine that comes out every other Friday)

What to Do if You're Not 21

Most places in New Orleans you have to be 18 or 19 (like Bruno's) to get in, so going to clubs and bars is not a problem even if you are underage. The only places that don't let underage people in are a majority of the strip clubs on Bourbon and a couple of bars on certain nights.

Local Specialties

Hurricanes, Hand Grenades, Frozen Daiquiris; TJ Quills has "the Orlando Magic" (which is a light blue concoction of pretty much every kind of Bacardi and grain alcohol)

Frats

See the Greek Section!

Students Speak Out On...
Nightlife

> **"Parties on campus are just like every other party, its all just alcohol and music. The bars are a nice break from school on a Friday night because they are close enough to campus that you will always see someone you know and you don't have to worry about a ride, you can walk."**

Q **"1st semester parties are good**, and always happening. Bourbon Street gets old. Some great bars are F&M's, Pat O'Brien's, The Red Rhino, and Jimmy's. The Boot is always a last resort."

Q "Parties on campus are a blast, the frats go all out. **Bars around campus are good, the ones around town are better,** but wherever you go in New Orleans, you're bound to have a good time! It's really fun to go see music at bars!"

Q **"Frat parties are pretty good – FREE BEER!** The bars and clubs around campus can be good for getting cheap drinks before going downtown. I personally am a fan of late night Boot, even if others aren't."

Q **"Here weekends start Tuesday night and last until Sunday**. Every night you'll end up at the Boot, but you can go to hundreds of places before. Thursday nights at F&M's are my favorite."

Q "Any on campus parties are probably lame, and off-campus parties usually revolve around drinking. **So if you like alcohol...come on down."**

Q "I don't know anything about the on campus scene, but **some good places to go off are The Maple Leaf, Mimi's in the Marigny, Delachaise**, etc...Where I go depends on my mood. Bars are diverse and plentiful."

Q "Parties on campus are theme parties at frat houses. There are numerous bars and clubs around the city. **My favorites are the Funky Butt and Twiropa.**"

Q **"There's always a party or something going on at the frat houses.** There are lots of local bars within walking distance, and the French Quarter is a cheap streetcar ride away."

The College Prowler Take On...
Nightlife

Living in New Orleans is like going to Disney World for a week – there's no way you can do everything that you want to do in your first year. There are many awesome bars and clubs in the city, and most let 18 and up through the door; they tend to serve drinks to whomever gets in.

Students agree that frat parties are the things to go at the beginning of the year in order to meet people, but going out to bars and clubs off campus is preferred. A lot go to bars that are in walking distance of Tulane, which have a large college clientele. If you want to go to the Quarter, it will only cost you $2.50 to get down and back, and there's always a street party going on down Bourbon (but mostly by tourists), and the clubs down there have good dance music, drink specials, and a lot of hotties.

The most popular place is The Boot, a bar that is across the street from Newcomb Hall and visible from JL. It's the place to meet up with all your friends before you head out on your night on the town, or the place to regroup after party hopping to all the frats. The happy hour on Friday nights is really popular, and it is usually packed until 9; after that, however, it's usually pretty empty until 2 or 3AM.

As a side note: believe in the freshman 15, my friend, and this is how you get it. People gain more weight here because of drinking a lot (especially beer) when they go out at night.

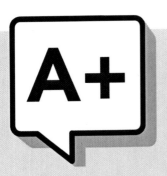

A+

The College Prowler™ Grade on

Nightlife: A+

A high grade in Nightlife indicates that there are many bars and clubs in the area that are easily accessible and affordable. Other determining factors include the number of options for the under-21 crowd and the prevalence of house parties.

Greek Life

The Lowdown On...
Greek Life

Number of Fraternities:

15

Number of Sororities:

9

Percent of Undergrad Men in Fraternities:

19%

Percent of Undergrad Women in Sororities:

33%

Fraternities on Campus:

Alpha Epsilon Pi
Alpha Phi Alpha
Alpha Tau Omega
Delta Tau Delta
Kappa Alpha
Kappa Alpha Psi
Kappa Sigma
Phi Beta Sigma
Phi Kappa Sigma
Sigma Alpha Epsilon
Sigma Alpha Mu
Sigma Chi
Sigma Phi Epsilon

→

Zeta Beta Tau
Zeta Psi

Sororities on Campus:

Alpha Epsilon Phi
Alpha Kappa Alpha
Alpha Omicron Pi
Chi Omega
Delta Sigma Theta
Delta Xi Nu
Kappa Alpha Theta
Kappa Kappa Gamma
Phi Beta Phi
Sigma Delta Tau
Zetta Phi Beta

Multicultural Colonies

Alpha Kappa Alpha
Alpha Phi Alpha
Delta Sigma Theta
Delta Xi Nu

Other Greek Organizations

Greek Council
Greek Peer Advisors
Interfraternity Council
Order of Omega
Panhellenic Council

Students Speak Out On...
Greek Life

> "It doesn't dominate at all. If you're in it, you can get into it and have fun with it. If you're not, it really doesn't matter. It can be a personal preference, which is cool."

Q "For me, **Greek Life does dominate the social scene**, however there are plenty of other things to do. There are lots of students that are not involved in Greek, but I feel like you gain access and knowledge of more parties."

Q "It dominates my social scene because I let it, and all of my good friends are in the same sorority and frat, but one could just as easily be a part of the same social scene without being in a sorority or frat. **Two of my good friends didn't pledge, and they are out with us every night."**

Q **"I am involved in Greek life, and I love it.** You can put as much time into it as you want, and it's not too intense. It does not dominate, and if you don't want to go Greek then it won't hinder your social life."

Q **"Greek Style? That's just a matter of preference.** I have never understood the whole hazing part."

Q "Greek life is very important for many people on campus. **I think it's a very dominating social crowd."**

Q **"There's plenty to do outside the Greek system."**

The College Prowler Take On...
Greek Life

If you go Greek, it will likely be a dominant part of your college life, but if you decide that it isn't your thing the Greek scene won't affect you at all. There is the option of going to frat and sorority parties during the fall semester, and the opportunity to rush and pledge in the spring semester. Other than being bombarded with people wearing Greek T-shirts, flip-flops, pins, etc., there is not much Greek on the Tulane campus.

People who are in fraternities and sororities are very loyal to their organization, and make it a priority right up there with schoolwork. You rarely ever hear of someone who is Greek hating the Greek system, and few leave fraternities/sororities once they've joined. Greek Life is a great way to make new friends, boyfriends and girlfriends, and connections for the future. Greek students tend to be fiercely loyal to their organizations and to their pledge groups, and many of these loyalties extend beyond the college years.

At Tulane, you won't feel pressured to join one of these organizations, and your social life isn't going to suffer if you choose to avoid pledging. Being in a sport or a club can provide almost the same network as any sorority or fraternity, and can be just as fun.

B

The College Prowler™ Grade on

Greek Life: B

A high grade in Greek Life indicates that sororities and fraternities are not only present, but also active on campus. Other determining factors include the variety of houses available and the respect the Greek community receives from the rest of the campus.

Drug Scene

The Lowdown On...
Drug Scene

Most Prevalent Drugs on Campus:
Alcohol
Marijuana
Cocaine

Liquor-Related Referrals:
46

Liquor-Related Arrests:
0

Drug-Related Referrals:
34

Drug-Related Arrests:
15

Drug Counseling Programs

Peer Health Advocates of Tulane (PHAT) – PHATs are Tulane student volunteers dedicated to raising awareness about various health issues facing college students. Though they aren't medical experts, these students are trained to provide information about abstinence, safe sex and contraception, nutrition, alcohol and drugs, and other health issues.

Students Speak Out On...
Drug Scene

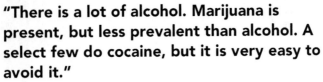

"There is a lot of alcohol. Marijuana is present, but less prevalent than alcohol. A select few do cocaine, but it is very easy to avoid it."

Q "It is definitely there, but not plainly out in the open. **When you go to any expensive private school, you get kids spending money on drugs."**

Q "Drugs are prevalent, but in no way an intricate part of social life. **As long as you know how to drink, you're good."**

Q "I hear a lot of talk about a lot of people doing coke, but I haven't seen it. **There's a pretty big dealing scene, mostly pot, and there are a lot of stoners here."**

Q "There's a ton of drinking going on and very little inter-vention. **We drink in the dorms and have only been warned once, even though we are loud."**

Q **"If you want something, it's accessible.** If you don't want to do them, it's not a big deal."

Q **"There's an abundance of weed,** but it's common every-where."

The College Prowler Take On...
Drug Scene

Other than marijuana and cocaine, there are not that many drugs that are heavily used on campus. However, alcohol is considered a drug, and a lot of students abuse it. Tulane EMS is constantly picking up people for alcohol poisoning, and there are plenty of drunks walking around on Thursday, Friday, and Saturday nights. If you don't like harder drugs then they are easily avoided, but trying to avoid the prevalence of alcohol is nearly impossible. Parties are dominated by kegs and shots, and when students go out it is usually to bars or clubs to drink. Tulane really does not have a strong drug/alcohol counseling service, and there has been concern about this recently because there is usually a student that overdoses on drugs each school year.

An important thing to remember, especially at Tulane, is that you can't assume who's involved in the drug scene. With any rich school, students have more money to buy drugs; intelligent, affluent students are just as likely as anyone else to be buying or selling drugs. Also, given a city like New Orleans, there's going to be a certain amount of substances – legal and otherwise – no matter where you go. Obviously you won't see people drinking in the middle of the day when walking on campus, but the weekends and nightlife are surrounded by alcohol.

The College Prowler™ Grade on
Drug Scene: C+

A high grade in the Drug Scene indicates that drugs are not a noticeable part of campus life; drug use is not visible, and no pressure to use them seems to exist.

Campus Strictness

The Lowdown On...
Campus Strictness

What Are You Most Likely to Get Caught Doing on Campus?

- Lighting candles/ incense in your room
- Trash/boxes left in the hallway
- Alcohol in your room (they look for this during fire drills)
- Having a microwave (it's against HRL policy, but everyone has one)
- Streaking
- Marijuana possession/smoking
- Parking or permit violations
- Drunk and disorderly behavior
- Noise violations
- Letting your boyfriend (or any guy in general) in the JL or Warren bathrooms or letting him walk around without an escort (if you're a girl, of course)
- Not having your card to swipe-in after 8PM (only some dorms)

Students Speak Out On...
Campus Strictness

"They don't care if they see you around at night and you are obviously drunk – they just want to make sure you are safe. If you are doing drugs in your dorm and you get caught, there are penalties."

Q **"It is strict.** I've heard of people getting expelled, but only if you get caught – which is avoidable for most people."

Q "Tulane is not at all. **It's New Orleans, it's like Disney World but with bars instead of rides."**

Q "They understand that kids will be kids, and **they let you off easy once for a minor infraction.** They are harder on you each subsequent time."

Q "Tulane is not strict at all. **If you are a raging drunk, they might give you a slap on the hand."**

Q **"The campus police aren't here to bust you**, they're just here to make sure you're safe."

Q "Drinking is not taken that seriously on campus. **If found with drugs, the consequences are a bit more severe**, but not what they make it out to be."

Q "Let me put it this way, I**'ve walked around with a microwave, a handle of tequila, and a bottle of rum in front of TUPD officers** that sit at the front desk at night."

The College Prowler Take On...
Campus Strictness

Not a day goes by that you don't see a TUPD officer on a bike, walking around campus, or manning the front desk of your dorm. It's strange to think that the police are so highly visible and yet relatively lax, but this is definitely the case at Tulane. Cops simply shake their heads when they see drunk and disorderly students, and do little to punish such behavior. The social life at Tulane is very dependent on alcohol, so they are used to seeing this kind of behavior year after year. New Orleans in general is very laid back when it comes to underage drinking; drugs are a different issue, however, both with the campus and the city. If students are caught possessing or dealing drugs, NOPD is called in and the consequences are serious. The minimum penalty for possession involves a referral to health services, community service work, and parental notification; you can even get expelled and arrested for possessing certain substances.

Oh, and as a side note: although they are pretty and you always wanted one as a child, you'll want to restrain yourself from petting the horses that the cops ride around on in the French Quarter. You can get in serious trouble for doing it.

A

The College Prowler™ Grade on

Campus Strictness: A

A high Campus Strictness grade implies an overall lenient atmosphere; police and RAs are fairly tolerant, and the administration's rules are flexible.

Parking

The Lowdown On...
Parking

Approximate Parking Permit Cost:

$275

Tulane Parking Services

Traffic Office, Tulane DPS

Phone: 865-5424

Web: http://www.tulane.edu/~dps/ (click on "Traffic")

Common Parking Tickets:

Failure to display a current Parking Permit while parked on Campus is $20.00 for the first offense, $50.00 for the second, and $75.00 for the third and following offenses

Parking too far from curb: $25.00 fine

Failure to obey officer: $75 fine and possible revocation of parking privileges for a year

Leaving scene of accident: $25 fine

Parking in "reserved all hours" or handicapped spots: $100 fine

Parking without permit in parking garage (during storm alert): $100 fine each day

→

Parking on sidewalk, loading zone: $30 fine

Speeding: $30-75 fine

Incomplete stop at stop sign; $30 fine

Expired meter: $10 for each half hour the meter has been expired; after 2 hours, car can be immobilized and the fine is then $100 a day

Student Parking Lot?

Yes

Freshman Allowed to Park?

No

Parking Permits

Parking Permits may be purchased at the Traffic Office on the ground floor of Diboll Complex, at Ben Weiner Drive and McAlister Extension. Hours are 8:30AM to 4PM Monday through Thursday, or Fridays 8:30AM to noon. You need a Tulane ID and your vehicle registration in hand when you go get one.

Did you know?

Best Places to Find a Parking Spot

Side streets off-campus

Good Luck Getting a Parking Spot Here!

Anywhere on campus that's not the huge parking garage next to Aron and Reily.

Students Speak Out On...
Parking

{ **"They oversell the spots in the parking garage, yet they expect everyone to be able to find a spot. Parking is definitely an issue."**

Q **"There is one garage which is far from dorms and the rest of campus,** but there are some street spots as well."

Q **"It is very hard to find parking on campus."**

Q **"There is NO parking!!"**

Q "When I come to school early, **I have to park 4 or 5 blocks away.** Good thing I carry a gun because I almost got held-up last semester walking to my car."

Q **"Parking permits are expensive and space is limited."**

Q "There doesn't appear to be a parking problem; the campus has a parking garage. However, **many people opt for bicycles for transportation on and off campus."**

The College Prowler Take On...
Parking

The garage on campus seems big, but you can never find a spot in it, and there is never anywhere to park on campus during the day. It is really easy to get a ticket on campus for parking in the wrong "color zone" or parking in a metered spot at night. City parking is only a little better – there are still many permit areas, timed spaces, and loading zones to watch out for, and it's easy to park in a bad area. There are also traffic cops all over the place, so even if you're staying somewhere for a few minutes, it's best to get a legal space.

Only upperclassmen can get parking permits, though there are always more cars with permits than there is space to park. A lot of freshman bring their cars to Tulane illegally and park on side streets off campus. Some constantly have to park 3 or 4 blocks away from campus, which can be not only inconvenient but also dangerous. Especially if you're leaving your car overnight (or returning to it in the dark), it's important to get a spot close to the university or in a safe neighborhood. All the spots aside from the garage and a few spots around campus are parallel, and this is also the case with most of the city itself – you'll need to know how to parallel park if you're bringing your car to New Orleans. Having a car can be a huge pain and expense, so this is something to seriously consider before coming to Tulane; the ability to go wherever you want is tempting, but the parking situation probably won't improve in the coming years.

C+

The College Prowler™ Grade on

Parking: C+

A high grade in this section indicates that parking is both available and affordable, and that parking enforcement isn't overly severe.

Transbortation

The Lowdown On...
Transportation

Ways to Get Around Town

On Campus

Tulane Uptown Square Shuttle Service

Monday-Thursday 7:40AM-5:15PM, Fridays until 5:55 PM. Goes to Uptown Square, Law Road at Herbert, and Fereret Street

Off/On-Campus Shuttle:

Operates every half hour with pickups at Gibson Circle, by the Navy ROTC Building, beside Rosen House, and at Howard-Tilton Library. Sunday-Thursday 5:15PM-2:10AM

Uptown/Downtown Shuttle:

This is a "commuting connection" between the Medical Center and the uptown campus. Monday-Friday 7AM-10:40PM, with stops at Reily, Rosen House, the Medical School, and the Tidewater building

Public Transportation

New Orleans Regional Transit Authority (NORTA, or RTA)

504-242-2600

Streetcars and buses run throughout the uptown area. Look on their website (http://

→

www.regionaltransit.org/) for
more information

Taxi Cabs

United Cabs Inc
1627 Polymnia Street
New Orleans, LA 70130
(504) 522-9771

Yellow-Checker Cab
3001 Conti Street
New Orleans, LA 70119

White Fleet Cabs
1629 Gentilly Boulevard
New Orleans, LA 70119
(504) 948-6605

Car Rentals

Alamo: local (504)469-0532
(800) 327-9633,
www.alamo.com

Avis: local: 504-464-9511,
(800) 831-2847, www.avis.com

Budget: local: 504-467-2277,
(800) 527-0700,
www.budget.com

Enterprise:
local: (504) 468-3018,
(800) 736-8222,
www.enterprise.com

Hertz: local: (504) 466-1237,
(800) 654-3131,
www.hertz.com

National: local: 504-466-4335,
(800) 227-7368,
www.nationalcar.com

Best Ways to Get Around Town

Cabs, the streetcar that runs
down St. Charles, bus, walking
Ways to Get
Out of Town

Airlines Serving New Orleans:

Air Canada , 1-888-247-2262,
www.aircanada.ca

Airtran, 1-800-AIR-TRAN,
www.airtran.com

American West Airlines,
800-2FLY-AWA,
www.americanwest.com

American Airlines,
(800) 433-7300,
www.americanairlines.com

Continental, (800) 523-3273,
www.continental.com

Delta, (800) 221-1212,
www.delta-air.com

Frontier, 1-800-432-1FLY,
www.frontierairlines.com

Jet Blue, (800) 538-2583,
www.jetblue.com

Northwest, (800) 225-2525,
www.nwa.com

Southwest, (800) 435-9792,
www.southwest.com

TWA, (800) 221-2000,
www.twa.com

US Airways, (800) 428-4322,
www.usairways.com

United, 1-800-864-8331,
www.ual.com

Grupo Taca,
www.grupotaca.com

Airport

Louis Armstrong International Airport

900 Airline Highway

Kenner, LA 70062

Phone: (504) 464-0831

Fax: (504) 465-1264

The airport is 11 miles from the Central Business District and approximately 16 miles from Tulane; it's a 30 minute drive in most cabs.

How to Get to the Airport

Airport Shuttle

$10 each way

504-522-3500 call for authorized pick-up and drop-off location

A Cab Ride to the Airport

Costs: $28.00 for one or two people, $12 for each additional person (up to 5)

Greyhound

For schedule information, call (800) 231-2222 or visit www.greyhound.com

Stops in New Orleans:

4.17 Miles from campus:

1001 Loyola Ave.

New Orleans LA 70113

(504) 524-7571

2 Limited bus stops at New Orleans Charity Hospital and the Louis Armstrong International Airport

Amtrak

The Amtrak Station is located in downtown, and is approximately 4.17 miles from campus. With an Amtrak Student Advantage Card, you get 15% off your rail fare to any of their destinations. Call (800) 872-7245 or visit www.Amtrak.com for schedule information.

New Orleans Amtrak Train Station

1001 Loyola Ave.

New Orleans, LA 70113

Travel Agents

STA Travel, Butler Hall First Floor (On Tulane Campus)

Open 9am-5pm Monday-Friday

(504) 865-5673

USA Travel Agency

1212 Saint Charles Ave

New Orleans, LA 70130

(504) 523-7818

Carrollton Travel Agency

4606 S Carrollton Ave

New Orleans, LA 70119

(504) 482-2295

Students Speak Out On...
Transportation

"It is not convenient or reliable at all. The only real means of transportation is streetcar, which is slow, unreliable, and only takes you to certain places. Taxis can be very expensive."

Q "Cabs are easy to get, but get expensive. The streetcar is cheap but slow and unreliable. I am too scared to use the bus."

Q "Public transportation is very convenient. The trolleys run all night for $1.25 one way per person."

Q "Transportation is not good at all! The street car is fine to get you to the French Quarter. Other places you can just walk to."

Q "It sucks! Public transportation is bad, scary, and a waste of my tax paying!"

Q "Taxi cabs are convenient, but expensive. The streetcar takes you downtown, but the ride lasts about 40 minutes each way. The bus is convenient for going to the grocery store."

Q "Cabs are too expensive to use all the time, and the streetcar is fun but unreliable."

Q "Public transportation is not as convenient as I'm used to (I grew up in Chicago). If you're looking into it, it's more available that you would initially perceive."

Q **"I have a love/ hate relationship with the streetcar.** Sometimes you have to wait 45 min. for one to come your way, and I never seem to have $1.25 with me, so I'm constantly buying gum at Rite Aid to get change."

Q **"There's no easy way to get to Wal-Mart or Target** (they are in Metairie)."

The College Prowler Take On...
Transportation

Though it's slow and not very dependable, public transportation is a cheap way to get around the city. Unless you want to take an expensive taxi ride or you meet someone with a car, say goodbye to commercial movie theaters, Target, and Wal-Mart. The closest are in Metairie, which is about a 20 minute drive from campus.

Streetcars are fun and new for about the first 5 times you ride them, but after that they're annoyingly slow and full of giddy tourists who wear parade beads in the middle of October. Although they actually do have a schedule, you'll rarely catch them on it – it's best to allow a lot of extra time if you're depending on them for anything. Fare is $1.25 for a one-way trip, and this gets you anywhere you need to go without the hassle of figuring out how much to pay. Buses also run through most of the city, and the fares are basically the same as on streetcars. Tulane's shuttle services around campus are dependable and come around frequently. They are also big coach busses, so it's a comfortable ride to wherever you're going.

Walking is always an option at Tulane, and usually is a pleasant one. A lot of locals jog down the St. Charles streetcar line day and night. Many students bring bikes and skateboards with them, and get around the city and campus that way. Overall, students have mixed feelings about public transportation; everyone would love to have their own car, but you can survive without one and do just fine in New Orleans.

B-

The College Prowler™ Grade on

Transportation: B-

A high grade for Transportation indicates that campus buses, public buses, cabs and rental cars are readily available and affordable. Other determining factors include proximity to an airport and the necessity of transportation.

Weather

The Lowdown On...
Weather

Average Temperature		Average Precipitation	
Fall:	71 °F	Fall:	4.65 in.
Winter:	56 °F	Winter:	4.94 in.
Spring:	70 °F	Spring:	5.11 in.
Summer:	83 °F	Summer:	6.53 in.

Students Speak Out On...
Weather

"The weather is generally warm with sporadic showers. You can depend on humidity and heat during spring, summer, and most of fall. Jeans and shorts are sufficient, along with a light jacket. Don't forget your umbrella!"

Q **"Weather, for the most part, is nice.** Pants or shorts with a tank top and a sweatshirt is almost always a safe bet."

Q **"Weather is so wonderful.** You get spoiled! Bring winter clothes, but not a lot. Bring tons of warm weather stuff and clothes to go out in!"

Q "I LOVE the weather. **I wear flip flops all year!"**

Q "The high temp. is high 80's, and the lowest would be low 40's. **Heavy winter clothes are not necessary, but bring an umbrella!"**

Q "It's generally nice and warm, although it does still get cold in the winter. **Bring an umbrella and a winter coat for sure."**

Q "Its always summer here. **Winters are really humid."**

Q **"It's just like Houston, so I'm used to it."**

Q **"The weather is absolutely gorgeous.** Bring clothing suitable for a wet climate. You may need a few sweaters and a jacket, but otherwise bring clothes suitable for 70 degree weather."

Q "Weather is excellent. Wear pants and a long sleeved shirt for cold weather, and make sure to bring a jacket. **In warm weather, you can wear anything you want."**

The College Prowler Take On...
Weather

Good news for all you Northerners: it never snows at Tulane. If it did, school would probably be closed because of the chaos that ensued. Hurricanes, however, are another matter entirely – there's always the looming threat during fall semester, and students hope for an evacuation to take time away from school. When it rains in New Orleans, it usually rains very hard; this is especially true in the springtime. Even winters are humid at Tulane, though the wind chill makes it feel colder than it really is. It's advisable to bring a jacket for the coldest months, though if you're used to Northern climates you'll survive in a hoodie and jeans.

New Orleans is a warm and sunny place most of the time, which welcomes frequent use of swimwear and summer clothes. You can wear flip flops during all seasons, but you'll also want an umbrella and galoshes – any rain that lasts for over 2 hours ensures the streets will be flooded.

The College Prowler™ Grade on

Weather: B+

A high Weather grade designates that temperatures are mild and rarely reach extremes, that the campus tends to be sunny rather than rainy, and that weather is fairly consistent rather than unpredictable.

Report Card Summary

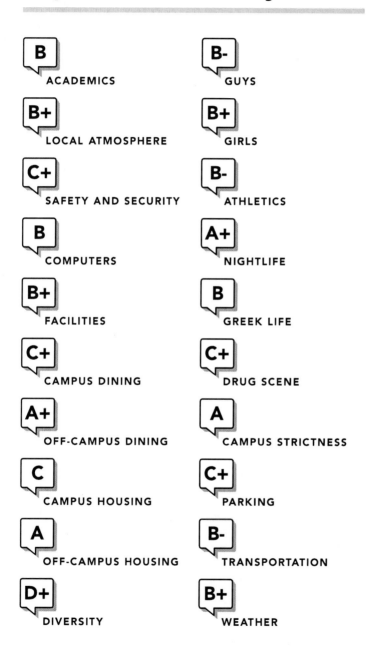

B
ACADEMICS

B-
GUYS

B+
LOCAL ATMOSPHERE

B+
GIRLS

C+
SAFETY AND SECURITY

B-
ATHLETICS

B
COMPUTERS

A+
NIGHTLIFE

B+
FACILITIES

B
GREEK LIFE

C+
CAMPUS DINING

C+
DRUG SCENE

A+
OFF-CAMPUS DINING

A
CAMPUS STRICTNESS

C
CAMPUS HOUSING

C+
PARKING

A
OFF-CAMPUS HOUSING

B-
TRANSPORTATION

D+
DIVERSITY

B+
WEATHER

Overall Experience

Students Speak Out On...
Overall Experience

{ **"I like where I am, and I don't want to be anywhere else. It takes some getting used to, but I like it."**

Q "My experience has been very good. **Difficult at times, amazing at others – a wide range of new experiences and emotions, which I think is a wonderful thing.** Overall, I'm very happy to be here. I think it's an ideal place to be for college for 4 years, and then move on. Coming here has enabled me to explore my interests in an inspiring, encouraging environment without little or no discouraging people or attitudes. I look forward to my next 3 years here, and I recommend Tulane to anyone who wants a unique college experience."

Q "If I were anywhere else, I would want to transfer. Other schools think they party, but Tulane is in a field of its own.

Going to school here is like living in another reality."

> "I love this school. **We appreciate the excellent opportunity we are given with the academics here**, but we know how to party. It's very laid back and fun."

> "I have truly enjoyed my first year; **opportunities were thrown my way, and I have met some very interesting people.** With my major in international relations and international development, I could not ask for more from a university."

> "I'm glad to be here. **It's a tough school, but I've had a lot of fun.** There weather is usually nice, so that makes me happy."

> **"As far as New Orleans, I would be nowhere else.** The name counts in school, so go to the best place you can. I wish I were at Harvard, but I couldn't take the weather or afford to live there."

> "I've really enjoyed my experiences thus far. No school is going to be perfect. I've definitely met some very interesting people, and **the setting of New Orleans as a college town makes it an amazing experience.** There's so much to do if you look for it. I'm happy where I am."

> "At first, I hated this school. I though that the people were shallow and drunk, the professors were below par, and I didn't like the New Orleans lifestyle at all. I couldn't find anyone who listened to music or liked going to the same things as I did. My first semester was really rough. However, once we got back from Christmas break, everything changed for the better. **I got more involved in things that I liked and I changed my major.** I had applied to transfer to another school for next year, but I'm staying here. Tulane just has to grow on you."

The College Prowler Take On...
Overall Experience

Tulane is an acquired taste. Some people take to it instantly, but for others it can take more than a semester to fit in and enjoy the university system. All of the students questioned said that they love Tulane and love being here. Living in such a culturally rich environment creates a unique learning opportunity that many kids who go to different schools will never get a chance to experience.

It takes a very intelligent and well-balanced person to attend Tulane. The nightlife and 24/7 party scene can tempt students to blow off classes and just have a good time. Finding the right balance of partying and school work makes for the best experience. Remember – this isn't high school glorified; college is actually going to be a lot of work. Even the so-called "blow off classes" that you take for humanities credit will make you read one longwinded book after the other, and write 10-15 page research papers by the end of the semester. You'll see a lot of people come in for the fall semester that won't come back after Christmas. Some people just can't take the pressure, others miss home too much. If you can get into Tulane, you can handle the workload; it's just that some adapt better than others. If you do have trouble, most professors are available to talk to, and the ERC's tutoring and writing workshops are free and easy to access.

You'll never sit at home on a weekend for lack of something to do, and holidays – especially Halloween and (obviously) Mardi Gras – are some of the best parts about living in New Orleans. The live jazz music and the food is also fantastic... If Bruff's food tasted like anything out in the city, the average student weight would be close to 300 pounds.

Not only will you get a well-balanced education at Tulane, but you will also meet some of your best friends, become involved in things you never imagined you would do at home, be a leader of a group when you never had that chance in high school, and be introduced to a new, unique environment and culture that can not be found in any other place in the country. There is no other school like Tulane, and there is no other city like New Orleans.

The Inside Scoop

The Lowdown On...
The Inside Scoop

Tulane Slang

Know the slang, know the school. The following is a list of things you really need to know before coming to Tulane. The more of these words you know, the better off you'll be.

The B-School: The Business School

The Beach/The Levy: The strip of land right next to the Mississippi River that is past Audubon Park. It is packed full of bikini clad women almost every weekend during spring semester.

Big Easy, The Rat, The Spawn of Rat: The Big Easy Café. Some people still live in the past and call the new late night place to eat "The Rat" (which was in the old UC until 2003)

Blackboard: Online board where teachers put up assignments, homework, and handouts for class

The Bubble: Otherwise known as the Pavilion. Has a food court and holds the bookstore.

The Deep: Part of the 3rd floor in JL hall

Downtown Campus: The

Medical School

The ERC: Educational Resources Center; free tutoring and a writing workshop

HRL: Housing and Residence Life Department

Mo: Monroe Hall

"Red Beans and Rice Day": Monday at Bruff

TOUR: Online registration

UC: University College

Uptown Campus: The undergrad campus on St. Charles

Things I Wish I Knew Before Coming to Tulane

- It's a big drinking school

- You actually can have a microwave

- Bruff sucks

- Greenbucks are worthless, go with the debit plan

- Orientation is crap, and you don't have to go

- Use the Roommate Finder (don't get a random roommate)

- Pay close attention to course listings and fulfillments (you can avoid some classes by taking others, depending on your major – look at requirements carefully!)

- Work load varies with your major (some are really hard, some easier)

- "Blow-off classes" are actually a lot of work

Tips to Succeed at Tulane

- Take classes that sound interesting – you'll hate yourself for taking something you have no interest in
- Balance partying with school!
- Go to class
- Learn how to parallel park
- Call your parents every now and again

- Do homework (more often than you call your parents, preferably)
- Go to the ERC if you need help, or ask a friend; there's no excuse to get confused
- Become good friends with your TA and RA
- Do laundry occasionally (wanting to do 6 loads at once is impossible)
- No, you can't do 16 shots
- Don't make it a goal to sleep with as many people as you can

Tulane Urban Legends

The third floor of JL (other wise known as the Deep) was the infirmary of Newcomb College back in the early days, but since then it has been used for single and double rooms. It is been known by all in JL to be haunted, and can be scary to go into at night.

A popular rumor is that sororities are outlawed on campus because local "brothel laws" prohibit more than a specified number of females from living together (in reality, this isn't true at all – in fact, Tulane students officially debunked this rumor in 1998 after researching New Orleans law as far back as 1800).

Students whose roommates commit suicide automatically receive a 4.0 grade point average for the current school term (another rumor that's taken hold at many schools).

School Spirit

For sports and other school sponsored events there is a lot of hype, but few students get incredibly excited. The bookstore sells Tulane shirts in every possible color and design, and they are very popular; you won't go a day without seeing someone with a Tulane sweatshirt or T-shirt on. Also, most people are very spirited about the specific organization that they are in – girls in sororities are always wearing a pin, a shirt, or even flip flops with their Greek letter on them, and people who play sports wear T-shirts that have their sport and number on them. When it comes to attending school events or cheering for sports teams, however, support tends to be few and far between.

Traditions

Commencement Day – graduates of all schools and colleges of the University march into the Louisiana Superdome, accompanied by banners, heralded by trumpet fanfares, moving to the music of Dr. Michael White's Original Liberty Jazz Band

Daisy Chain – a ritual at commencement and Newcomb Convocation where a select group of Newcomb juniors, dressed in white, carry a chain of daisies.

Oak Wreath – a special dinner at the residence of the Newcomb Dean, held for senior women who are recognized for their contributions to the college.

Senior Salute – a formal reception at the Newcomb Dean's residence to recognize all graduating seniors prior to commencement.

Newcomb Awards Ceremony – designed to recognize Newcomb students for academic excellence and leadership on Newcomb's campus and at Tulane as a whole.

Homecoming game – The football game is always played in Tad Gormley Stadium

Nicknames – "Green Wave," "Greenbacks," and "Greenies" were created because of the color of the football jerseys

Finding a Job or Internship

The Lowdown On...
Finding a Job or Internship

It is really easy to get work study at Tulane. A lot of people work at Reily, the front desk of their dorm, or a department in one of the colleges. Already for the 2004-2005 school year Tulane has planned to have 5 career fairs, and more will come up as the year progresses.

Advice

Go to the career fairs that are on campus. You can get information about businesses around the area, nonprofit programs that need interns, and even jobs at Tulane itself.

Apply for more than one internship because chances are you won't get the first one you apply for. Most importantly – apply early. A lot of places have applications for summer internships due in November.

Career Center Resources & Services

The Tulane Career Services Center: offers information on local, national and international internships in binders and publications located in the Career Library.

Phone: 504.865.5107
Email: csc@tulane.edu

ASCNET: Tulane's contacts with alumni in career fields (through the Career services).

The Career Services CyberCenter Information for Students: links to Job Search Engines.

Internship Exchange: a consortium of a dozen universities offering thousands of internships worldwide

Alumni

The Lowdown On...
Alumni

Website:
http://alumni.tulane.edu/

Office:
Tulane Alumni Affairs
6319 Willow
New Orleans, LA 70118
504-865-5901 or 877-4TU-LANE

Services Available

Clubs: AAC (Alumni Admissions Committee), BANTU (Multicultural), The Emeritus Club (Members of 50 year and earlier classes and Emeritus faculty), Green Pride (gay and lesbian), Heath and Science Center Alumni, Newcomb Alumnae, Orleans Batillion ROTC, Society of Tulane Engineers, T Club (athletes), TABA (Tulane Association of Business Alumni), TAA (Tulane Alumni Association), Tulane International Alumni, Tulane Law Alumni, Tulane Naval ROTC Alumni Assocation, and there are Tulane Clubs based in all the major cities in the US.

Tulane Alumni Association Membership Card: alumni can use this card for discounts at some campus stores and for access to selected campus

→

facilities such as the library, career services, and the fitness center.

Insurance Services: Medical Insurance, Life Insurance, Auto, Homeowner's, and Renter's insurance are available.

Restaurant, Travel, and Shopping Discounts

Ability to have a Tulane University Credit Card

Permanent E-Mail Forwarding

Alumni Locator

"Tulane Alumni Preferred Golfers Club at Eastover" (check out http://www.eastovercc.com for more information)

Affiliate membership in the Cornell Club of New York (http://www.cornellclubnyc.com)

Alumni Travel Program (call 1-877-4-TULANE and ask for Alison Walsh)

The Princeton Review New Orleans Office: 10% discount on all review courses (this discount extends to spouses and children of alumni); to register call (504) 865-1060

Major Alumni Events

Travel: each year, alumni have the opportunity to go on trips worldwide with former classmates. Most trips are guided by a faculty member with expertise in the region.

City club "Crawfish Boils"

Class reunions

Homecoming events and planning

TAA Board meeting weekend

Alumni Publications

The Tulanian

A quarterly magazine for alumni that has features about students, life at Tulane and the surrounding area.

Famous Alumni

Neil Bush (bachelor's in 1977, MBA 1979) – Younger brother of President George W. Bush

Jerry Springer (1965) – Talk show host

Robert Steinberg (1981) – Actor

Bruce Paltrow (1965) – Director, father of Gwyneth Paltrow

Newt Gingrich (masters in 1968, PhD in 1971) – Republican Congressional representative from Georgia

Shirley Ann Grau (1965) – winner of the Pulitzer Prize for her work The Keepers of the House

John Kennedy Toole (1981) – winner of the Pulitzer Prize for his work The Confederacy of Dunces

Student Organizations

Student Organizations

Undergraduate Student Government,
www.tulane.edu/%7Eusg/

Ballroom Dancing

Baseball Club

Capoeira Angola Club of Tulane

Climbing Club

Cricket Club

Fencing Club

Field Hockey Club

Gymnastics Club

Ice Hockey, www.tulanehockey.com

Judo Club, www.tulane.edu/~judo

Karate Club

Men's Lacrosse Club

Women's Lacrosse Club

Martial Arts Club, www.tulane.edu/~martial

Rock Climbing Club

Rowing Club, www.tulane.edu/~martial

Men's Rugby Club, www.tulane.edu/~rugby/

Running Club, www.tulane.edu/~running/

Sailing Club

Men's Soccer Club
Women's Soccer Club
Swimming Club
Tennis Club
Tulane Dodgeball Club
Tulane Runners Club
Tulane SCUBA Club
Tulane Waterski Club
Ultimate Frisbee Club, www.tuluultimate.com
Women's Ultimate Frisbee Club
Volleyball Club, www.tulane.edu/~volleyb/
Water Polo Club
Waterski Club
Alpha Kappa Psi, www.tulane.edu/~akpsi
Anthropology Student Union of Tulane
Green Wave Ambassadors
National Society of Black Engineers, www.tulane.edu~nsbe
Peer Health Advocates
Pi Sigma Alpha
Rape Emergency Awareness and Coping Hot Line
Student Admission Committee
Student Health Advisory Committee
Toastmasters
Tulane College Leadership Caucus
Honor Societies:
Alpha Lambda Delta
Financial Management Association
Omega Chi Epsilon (Chemical Engineering)
Omicron Delta Kappa, www.tulane.edu/~odk/
Order of Omega (Fraternity and Sorority)
Phi Alpha Theta
Phi Sigma Pi
Psi Chi, www.tulane.edu/~psichi/psychclub.htm
Tau Beta Pi (Engineering)
The William Wallace Peery Society
Tulane Engineering and Computer Science Honors Society
American Institute of Architecture Students
American Institute of Chemical Engineers, www.tulane.edu/~aiche
American Society of Mechanical Engineers,
www.asme.org/students/

Association of Computing Machinists
Association of Liberal Arts/Pre-professional Organizations
Association of Pre-Dental Students
Biomedical Engineering Society
Freeman Consulting Group, www.freeman.tulane.edu/fcg
Institute of Electrical and Electronics Engineers
Interdisciplinary Scholars Network
Philosophy Club
Pre law Society, www.tulane.edu/~prelaw
Pre medical Society
Psychology Club, www.tulane.edu/~psichi/psychclub.htm
Society of Automotive Engineers
Society of Hispanic Professional Engineers
Society of Women Engineers
Spanish and Portuguese Student Association
Tulane Anthropology Student Union of Tulane
Tulane Exercise and Sports Science Society
Tulane Investors Group
Tulane University Latin American Studies Organization
Tulane University Neuroscience Association
Tulane University Paralegal Association, www.tulane.edu/~tupa
Tulane-Newcomb Art Student Association
Women In Science
Media Board
The Pier Glass, www.tulane.edu/~pier
The Tulane Hullabaloo, www.thehullabaloo.com
Tulane Jambalaya Yearbook, www.tulane.edu/~jam/
Tulane Literary Society
Tulane Review
Tulane Student Television
WTUL
Air Force Reserve Officer Training Corp
African-American Congress of Tulane, www.tulane.edu/~act
Asian American Students United, www.tulane.edu/~aasu
Celtic Society, www.tulane.edu/~celtic
Indian Association of Tulane University, www.tulane.edu/~iatu
International Student Association of Tulane
Latin and American Student Association
Mexican Students of Tulane

Middle Eastern Student Association

Multicultural Council

Muslim Educational and Cultural Committee for Awareness

Muslim Student Association

Students Organized Against Racism (SOAR)

Tulane African Student Association

Tulane Chinese Student Association (ROC), www.tulane.edu/~taiwan/

Tulane Chinese Students & Scholars Association(PRC), www.tulane.edu/~tcssa

Tulane University Vietnamese Association

Turkish Student Organization

ACLU

College Democrats

College Republicans

Free the Planet

Political Advocacy League

Tulane Campus Libertarians

Tulane Politics Club

Young Democrats of Tulane University

Tulane-Israel Public Affairs Committee, www.tulane.edu/%7Ehillel/tipac.swf

Association of Programming and Performance Organizations, http://www.tulane.edu/~appo/

Cheerleaders

Green Envy (choir), www.Green-Envy.org

Jump, Jive and Wave Tulane Swing Dance Club

Model United Nations

Shockwave (dance team), www.tulane.edu/~shockwave

Soundwave (band), www.tulane.edu/~soundw

Student Alumni Ambassadors

THEM (acapella singing group), www.tulane.edu/~them/

TsUnami

Tulane College Bowl

Tulane Forensics Team

Tulane University Campus Programming, www.tucp.net

Chi Alpha Christian Fellowship

Club Paintball

Communication Majors Society

Feminist Majority Leadership Alliance (FMLA), www.feministcampus.org

International Game Developers Association (IGDA), www.tulane.edu/~igda/

Men of Color

Orthodox Christian Fellowship (OCF)

TURBO (robotics), www.eecs.tulane.edu/TURBO

Tulane Anime and Manga Society

Tulane Music Organization

Tulane Second Line Club

Tulane University Mac Users Group, tumug.tulane.edu

World Affairs Forum

Baptist Collegiate Ministry

Catholic Center, www.tulanecatholic.org/main.htm

Chabad House

Christian Medical and Dental Society

Episcopal Student Ministry

InterVarsity Christian Fellowship

New Orleans Hillel Center, www.neworleanshillel.org

Presbyterian, Disciples and United Church of Christ

Tulane Lutheran Ministry

United Campus Ministries

United Methodist Campus Center

Association of Service and Education Organizations

Circle K International

Community Action Council of Tulane University Students, www.tulane.edu/~cactus

Green Club

MOSAIC

Newcomb Assets

Residence Hall Association

Stand For Children

Town Students Association

Tulane Emergency Medical Service (TEMS), www.tulaneems.com

Tulane Meditation Club

Tulane Men Against Rape

TULAP

Architecture Student Body

Associated Student Body

Engineering Student Council

Freeman Student Government

Newcomb College Senate

Tulane College Senate

USG Tidal Wave Homecoming Committee

University College Student Government Association

The Best & The Worst

The Ten BEST Things About Tulane:

1. Location (can't get any better than New Orleans)
2. Never gets below 40 degrees, and it never snows
3. Free cable and fast Internet
4. Small campus (a walk across campus takes about 10 minutes)
5. Lack of strictness with drinking
6. Overabundance of clubs and organizations
7. The food (off campus)
8. The unique culture
9. There's always something to do
10. Broad range of interesting classes, and the ability to take classes at Loyola next door

The Ten **WORST** Things About Tulane:

1. UC/new dorm construction
2. The sheer amount of drinking and partying
3. The rain
4. The food (on campus)
5. The slowest mailroom on earth
6. Tuition costs
7. High cost of recreation in New Orleans
8. Classes fill up really fast, and it's impossible for a lot of people to get into lab times for upper-level classes
9. High crime rates in the areas surrounding campus
10. The incessant beeping of maintenance and police golf carts around campus

Visiting Tulane

The Lowdown On...
Visiting Tulane

Hotel Information
Closest to campus, on the St. Charles Streetcar line:

Avenue Plaza Hotel
2111 St. Charles
(504) 566-1212
Price Range: $100-120

Hampton Inn
3626 St. Charles
(504) 899-9990
Price Range: $70

Pontchartrain Hotel
2031 St. Charles
(504) 524-0581
Price Range: $60-300

Quality Inn - Maison St. Charles
1319 St. Charles
(504) 522-0187
Price Range: $95-110

Bienville House Hotel
320 Decatur St.
(504) 529-2345
Price Range: $130-150

www.collegeprowler.com

Doubletree Hotel
300 Canal St.
(504) 581-1300
Price Range: $200-300

Holiday Inn French Quarter
124 Royal St.
(504) 529-7211
Price: $110-130

Hotel Inter-Continental
444 St. Charles
(504) 525-5566
Price Range: $180-2000

Hyatt Regency Hotel
500 Poydras Plaza
(504) 561-1234
Price Range: $115- 170

Le Pavillon Hotel
833 Poydras St.
(504)581-3111
Price Range: $130-230

Marriott
555 Canal St.
(504) 581-1000
Price range: $130-200

Omni Royal Orleans
621 St. Louis St.
(504) 529-5333
Price Range: $145-450

Royal Sonesta
300 Bourbon St.
(504) 586-0300
Price Range: $150-400

Sheraton New Orleans
500 Canal St.
(504) 525-2500

W New Orleans
333 Poydras Street
(504) 525-9444
Price Range: $150-180

Take a Campus Virtual Tour

Virtual Tour: *http://www2.tulane.edu/about_tour.cfm*

Buy a video: *http://www.videc.com/videoidx.cfm*

Campus Tours

Tulane welcomes visitors in the Undergraduate Admission Office, Room 210 Gibson Hall. Information sessions and campus tours begin at 9:00 am and 2:00 pm Monday through Friday, and at 9:00 am on most Saturdays during the school year.

To Schedule a Group Information Session or Interview:

Call the Undergraduate Admissions Office between 8:30 am and 5:00 pm at (504) 865 - 5731 or (800) 873 – 9283.

Inside Tulane:

Is a program held on Saturdays each fall which includes presentations by Admission and Financial Aid staff, faculty, and students, as well as a campus tour.

Tulane Days:

This program is designed for accepted students; sessions are held on weekdays through March and April.

Overnight Visits

Prospective students can spend a night in a dorm with a current student any Sunday through Thursday evening while classes are in session. You'll be scheduled for a campus tour, and may be able to attend a class as well. Additionally, you'll get a complimentary meal and a guest pass to the Reily Recreation Center. Call the Office of Undergraduate Admission at least two weeks in advance to schedule this type of visit; hours are Monday through Friday between 8:30AM and 5PM; the number is (800) 873-9283 (Fax: (504) 862-8715).

Directions to Campus

Driving from the East

FROM I-10, going East; follow the signs toward the Central Business District. Take Carrollton Avenue exit. Follow South Carrollton until shortly before it ends, and turn left on St. Charles Avenue. Tulane and Gibson Hall will be on your left at 6823 St. Charles Avenue. Gibson Hall is the center of the three main stone buildings on St. Charles Avenue. Proceed up the center staircase, and you will be right at the undergraduate Admission Office.

Driving from the West

FROM I-10 going West; as you enter the downtown area, follow the signs to Hwy. 90 Business/West Bank. Exit at St. Charles Avenue/Carondelet Street (do not cross the bridge). At the second traffic light make a right turn onto St. Charles Avenue. Follow St. Charles Avenue for four miles. Tulane and Gibson Hall will be on your right at 6823 St. Charles Avenue.

Words to Know

Academic Probation – A student can receive this if they fail to keep up with their school's academic minimums. Those who are unable to improve their grades after receiving this warning can possibly face dismissal.

Beer Pong / Beirut – A drinking game with numerous cups of beer arranged in a particular pattern on each side of a table. The goal is to get a ping pong ball into one of the opponent's cups by throwing the ball or hitting it with a paddle. If the ball lands in a cup, the opponent is required to drink the beer.

Bid – An invitation from a fraternity or sorority to pledge their specific house.

Blue Light Phone – Brightly-colored phone posts with a blue light bulb on top. These phones exist for security purposes and are located at various outside locations around most campuses. If a student has an emergency or is feeling endangered, they can pick up one of these phones (free of charge) to connect with campus police or an escort service.

Campus Police – Policemen who are specifically assigned to a given institution. Campus police are not regular city officers; they are employed by the university in a full-time capacity.

Club Sports – A level of sports that falls somewhere between varsity and intramural. If a student is unable to commit to a varsity team but has a lot of passion for athletics, a club sport could be a better, less intense option. If a club sport still requires too much commitment, intramurals often involve no traveling and a lot less time.

Cocaine – An illegal drug. Also known as "coke" or "blow," cocaine often resembles a white crystalline or powdery substance. It is highly addictive and dangerous.

Common Application – An application that students can use to apply to multiple schools.

Course Registration – The time when a student selects what courses they would like for the upcoming quarter or semester. Prior to registration, it is best to have an idea of several back-up courses in case a particular class becomes full. If a course is full, a student can place themselves on the waitlist, although this still does not guarantee entry.

Division Athletics – Athletics range from Division I to Division III. Division IA is the most competitive, while Division III is considered to be the least competitive.

Dorm – Short for dormitory, a dorm is an on-campus housing facility. Dorms can provide a range of options from suite-style rooms to more communal options that include shared bathrooms. Most first-year students live in dorms. Some upperclassmen who wish to stay on campus also choose this option.

Early Action – A way to apply to a school and get an early acceptance response without a binding commitment. This is a system that is becoming less and less available.

Early Decision – An option that students should use only if they are positive that a place is their dream school. If a student applies to a school using the early decision option and is admitted, they are required and bound to attend that university. Admission rates are usually higher with early decision students because the school knows that a student is making them their first choice.

Ecstasy – An illegal drug. Also known as "e" or "x," ecstasy looks like a pill and most resembles an aspirin." Considered a party drug, ecstasy is very dangerous and can be deadly.

Ethernet – An extremely fast internet connection that is usually available in most university-owned residence halls. To use an Ethernet connection properly, a student will need a network card and cable for their computer.

Fake ID – A counterfeit identification card that contains false information. Most commonly, students get fake IDs and change their birthdates so that they appear to be older than 21 (of legal drinking age). Even though it is illegal, many college students have fake IDs in hopes of purchasing alcohol or getting into bars.

Frosh – Slang for "freshmen."

Hazing – Initiation rituals that must be completed for membership into some fraternities or sororities. Numerous universities have outlawed hazing due to its degrading or dangerous requirements.

Sports (IMs) – A popular, and usually free, student activity where students create teams and compete against other groups for fun. These sports vary in competitiveness and can include a range of activities—everything from billiards to water polo. IM sports are a great way to meet people with similar interests.

Keg – Officially called a half barrel, a keg contains roughly 200 12-ounce servings of beer and is often found at college parties.

LSD – An illegal drug. Also known as acid, this hallucinogenic drug most commonly resembles a tab of paper.

Marijuana – An illegal drug. Also known as weed or pot; besides alcohol, marijuana is one of the most commonly-found drugs on campuses across the country.

Major –The focal point of a student's college studies; a specific topic that is studied for a degree. Examples of majors include physics, English, history, computer science, economics, business, and music. Many students decide on a specific major before arriving on campus, while others are simply "undecided" and figure it out later. Those who are extremely interested in two areas can also choose to double major.

Meal Block – The equivalent of one meal. Students on a "meal plan" usually receive a fixed number of meals per week.

Each meal, or "block," can be redeemed at the school's dining facilities in place of cash. More often than not, if a student fails to use their weekly allotment of meal blocks, they will be forfeited.

Minor – An additional focal point in a student's education. Often serving as a compliment or addition to a student's main area of focus, a minor has fewer requirements and prerequisites to fulfill than a major. Minors are not required for graduation from most schools; however some students who want to further explore many different interests choose to have both a major and a minor.

Mushrooms – An illegal drug. Also known as "shrooms," this drug looks like regular mushrooms but are extremely hallucinogenic.

Off-Campus Housing – Housing from a particular landlord or rental group that is not affiliated with the university. Depending on the college, off-campus housing can range from extremely popular to non-existent. Those students who choose to live off campus are typically given more freedom, but they also have to deal with things such as possible subletting scenarios, furniture, and bills. In addition to these factors, rental prices and distance often affect a student's decision to move off campus.

Office Hours – Time that teachers set aside for students who have questions about the coursework. Office hours are a good place for students to go over any problems and to show interest in the subject material.

Pledging – The time after a student has gone through rush, received a bid, and has chosen a particular fraternity or sorority they would like to join. Pledging usually lasts anywhere from one to two semesters. Once the pledging period is complete and a particular student has done everything that is required to become a member, they are considered a brother or sister. If a fraternity or a sorority would decide to "haze" a group of students, these initiation rituals would take place during the pledging period.

Private Institution – A school that does not use taxpayers dollars to help subsidize education costs. Private schools typically cost more than public schools and are usually smaller.

Prof – Slang for "professor."

Public Institution – A school that uses taxpayers dollars to help subsidize education costs. Public schools are often a good value for in-state residents and tend to be larger than most private colleges.

Quarter System (sometimes referred to as the Trimester System) – A type of academic calendar system. In this setup, students take classes for three academic periods. The first quarter usually starts in late September or early October and concludes right before Christmas. The second quarter usually starts around early to mid–January and finishes up around March or April. The last quarter, or "third quarter," usually starts in late March or early April and finishes up in late May or Mid-June. The fourth quarter is summer. The major difference between the quarter system and semester system is that students take more courses but with less coverage.

RA (Resident Assistant) – A student leader who is assigned to a particular floor in a dormitory in order to help to the other students who live there. A RA's duties include ensuring student safety and providing guidance or assistance wherever possible.

Recitation – An extension of a specific course; a "review" session of sorts. Because some classes are so large, recitations offer a setting with fewer students where students can ask questions and get help from professors or TAs in a more personalized environment. As a result, it is common for most large lecture classes to be supplemented with recitations.

Rolling Admissions – A form of admissions. Most commonly found at public institutions, schools with this type of policy continue to accept students throughout the year until their class sizes are met. For example, some schools begin accepting students as early as December and will continue to do so until April or May.

Room and Board – This is typically the combined cost of a university-owned room and a meal plan.

Room Draw/Housing Lottery – A common way to pick on-campus room assignments for the following year. If a student decides to remain in university-owned housing, they are assigned a unique number that, along with seniority, is used to choose their new rooms for the next year.

Rush – The period in which students can meet the brothers and sisters of a particular chapter and find out if a given fraternity or sorority is right for them. Rushing a fraternity or a sorority is not a requirement at any school. The goal of rush is to give students who are serious about pledging a feel for what to expect.

Semester System – The most common type of academic calendar system at college campuses. This setup typically includes two semesters in a given school year. The "fall" semester starts around the end of August or early September and finishes right before winter vacation. The "spring" semester usually starts in mid-January and ends around late April or May.

Student Center/Rec Center/Student Union – A common area on campus that often contains study areas, recreation facilities, and eateries. This building is often a good place to meet up with fellow students and is most commonly used as a hangout. Depending on the school, the student center can have a huge role or a non-existent role in campus life.

Student ID – A university-issued photo ID that serves as a student's key to many different functions within an institution. Some schools require students to show these cards in order to get into dorms, libraries, cafeterias, and other facilities. In addition to storing meal plan information, in some cases, a student ID can actually work as a debit card and allow students to purchase things from bookstores or local shops.

Suite – A type of dorm room. Unlike other places that have communal bathrooms that are shared by the entire floor, a suite has a private bathroom. Suite-style dorm rooms can house anywhere from two to ten students.

TA (Teacher's Assistant) – An undergraduate or grad student who helps in some manner with a specific course. In some cases, a TA will teach a class, assist a professor, grade assignments, or conduct office hours.

Undergraduate – A student who is in the process of studying for their Bachelor (college) degree.

ABOUT THE AUTHOR:

Born in raised in Houston, Texas, Kate Dearing joined the Tulane Community in the fall of 2003 after graduating with honors from Langham Creek High School. She is currently a double major of communications and Spanish in the Newcomb College, the secretary of the women's ultimate Frisbee team, and one of the news editors for the Tulane Hullabaloo.

I'd like to thank all my lab rats (a.k.a. Tulanians) who made this possible. Thank you to all my moms and dads, all my siblings, my favorite cousin Jillian who left science for Spanish (good choice), all my friends from past and present—especially Sunny and Elaine who were the ones to get me through my first year, and for all the people here at Tulane who have made my first year at college something I'll never forget. This book is dedicated to my best friend Stan, who has always believed in me more than I've ever believed in myself.

Dear reader,

I leave you now with some advice that I've learned while being here. Get involved. I know of so many kids who came here and left after 1st semester because they didn't feel like they were a part of the community. Go out there and play a sport you have never played (like ultimate Frisbee, perhaps), or join a religious or culture group to understand something you were never exposed to back at home. Make friends and enemies. This is a part of your life that you will always look back on and wish you were still there. Take advantage of what it has to offer. Good luck with all that senior year includes, and hopefully I'll see you in the fall.

Cheers,

Kate Dearing

P.S. If you have any questions, comments, or perhaps donations, email me at katedearing@collegeprowler.com I love mail, so send some my way.

Notes

Notes

....

....

....

....

....

....

....

....

....

....

....

....

....

Notes

....

....

....

....

....

....

....

....

....

....

....

....

....

....

Notes

....

....

....

....

....

....

....

....

....

....

....

....

....

Notes

....

....

....

....

....

....

....

....

....

....

....

....

....

Notes

....

....

....

....

....

....

....

....

....

....

....

....

....

Notes

Notes

....

....

....

....

....

....

....

....

....

....

....

....

Notes

....

....

....

....

....

....

....

....

....

....

....

....

....

Notes

....

....

....

....

....

....

....

....

....

....

....

....

....

Notes

Notes

....

....

....

....

....

....

....

....

....

....

....

....

....

Notes

....

....

....

....

....

....

....

....

....

....

....

....

....

Notes

....

....

....

....

....

....

....

....

....

....

....

....

....

Notes

....

....

....

....

....

....

....

....

....

....

....

....

....

Notes

....

....

....

....

....

....

....

....

....

....

....

....

....

Notes

....

....

....

....

....

....

....

....

....

....

....

....

....

Notes

....

....

....

....

....

....

....

....

....

....

....

....

....

Notes

....

....

....

....

....

....

....

....

....

....

....

....

....

Need More Help?

Do you have more questions about this school? Can't find a certain statistic? College Prowler is here to help. We are the best source of college information on the planet. We have a network of thousands of students who can get the latest information on any school to you ASAP. E-mail us at *info@collegeprowler.com* with your college-related questions. It's like having an older sibling show you the ropes!

Email Us Your College-Related Questions!

Check out **www.collegeprowler.com** for more details.
1.800.290.2682

Notes

....

....

....

....

....

....

....

....

....

....

....

....

....

Tell Us What Life Is Really Like At Your School!

Have you ever wanted to let people know what your school is really like? Now's your chance to help millions of high school students choose the right school.

Let your voice be heard and win cash and prizes!

Check out **www.collegeprowler.com** for more info!

Notes

Do You Have What It Takes To Get Admitted?

The College Prowler Road to College Counseling Program is here. An admissions officer will review your candidacy at the school of your choice and create a 12+ page personal admission plan. We rate your credentials with the same criteria used by school admissions committees. We assess your strengths and weaknesses and create a plan of action that makes a difference.

Check out **www.collegeprowler.com** or call 1.800.290.2682 for complete details.

Notes

....

....

....

....

....

....

....

....

....

....

....

....

....

Pros and Cons

Still can't figure out if this is the right school for you?
You've already read through this in-depth guide; why not
list the pros and cons? It will really help with narrowing down
your decision and determining whether or not
this school is right for you.

Pros	Cons

Notes

Need Help Paying For School?

Apply for our Scholarship!

College Prowler awards thousands of dollars a year to students who compose the best essays. E-mail *scholarship@collegeprowler.com* for more information, or call 1.800.290.2682.

Apply now at **www.collegeprowler.com**

Notes

Get Paid To Rep Your City!

Make money for college!

Earn cash by telling your friends about College Prowler!

Excellent Pay + Incentives + Bonuses

Compete with reps across the nation for cash bonuses

Gain marketing and communication skills

Build your resume and gain work experience for future career opportunities

Flexible work hours; make your own schedule

Opportunities for advancement

Contact *sales@collegeprowler.com*
Apply now at **www.collegeprowler.com**

Notes

....

....

....

....

....

....

....

....

....

....

....

....

....

Do You Own A Website?

Would you like to be an affiliate of one of the fastest-growing companies in the publishing industry? Our web affiliates generate a significant income based on customers whom they refer to our website. Start making some cash now! Contact *sales@collegeprowler.com* for more information or call 1.800.290.2682

Apply now at **www.collegeprowler.com**

Notes

....

....

....

....

....

....

....

....

....

....

....

....

....

Notes

Write For Us!

Get Published! Voice Your Opinion.

Writing a College Prowler guidebook is both fun and rewarding; our open-ended format allows your own creativity free reign. Our writers have been featured in national newspapers and have seen their names in bookstores across the country. Now is your chance to break into the publishing industry with one of the country's fastest-growing publishers!

Apply now at **www.collegeprowler.com**

Contact *editor@collegeprowler.com* or call 1.800.290.2682 for more details.

Notes

....

....

....

....

....

....

....

....

....

....

....

....

....

Notes

....

....

....

....

....

....

....

....

....

....

....

....

....

Notes

....

....

....

....

....

....

....

....

....

....

....

....

....

Notes

....
....
....
....
....
....
....
....
....
....
....
....
....

Notes

....

....

....

....

....

....

....

....

....

....

....

....

....

Notes

....

....

....

....

....

....

....

....

....

....

....

....

....